THE FACE OF HUNGER

THE FACE OF HUNGER

Reflections on a Famine in Ethiopia

BYRON CONNER, M.D.

ReadersMagnet, LLC

The Face of Hunger
Copyright © 2019 by Byron Conner, M.D.

Published in the United States of America
ISBN Paperback: 978-1-950947-65-2
ISBN Hardback: 978-1-950947-66-9
ISBN eBook: 978-1-950947-67-6

All rights reserved. No part of this publication may be reproduced, stored in a retrieval system or transmitted in any way by any means, electronic, mechanical, photocopy, recording or otherwise without the prior permission of the author except as provided by USA copyright law.

The opinions expressed by the author are not necessarily those of ReadersMagnet, LLC.

ReadersMagnet, LLC
10620 Treena Street, Suite 230 | San Diego, California, 92131 USA
1.619.354.2643 | www.readersmagnet.com

Book design copyright © 2019 by ReadersMagnet, LLC. All rights reserved.
Cover design by Ericka Walker
Interior design by Shieldon Watson

Dedication

To those who survived, wherever they may be

To my wife: Alfredia and children: Kellie and Kevin, who shared so much of this experience with me

Famine

A severe shortage of food resulting in widespread hunger and starvation

"For nation shall rise against nation, and kingdom against kingdom: and there shall be famines, and pestilences, and earthquakes, in diver's places."

—Matthew 24:7

And if thou draw out thy soul to the hungry, and satisfy the afflicted soul; then shall thy light rise in obscurity and thy darkness be as noon day.

—Isaiah 58:10

Acknowledgments

I would like to express my gratitude to numerous individuals, churches and humanitarian organizations that had an impact on my life and work as follows:

- My wife and children because of their wonderful companionship
- My numerous siblings, cousins, uncles, aunts, nieces, and nephews that make me thankful I have such a large family
- The Park Hill Seventh-day Adventist Church that has given me spiritual nurturing since I was 9 years of age.
- The late Dr. Rene Evard, the dean of admissions at the Loma Linda University School of Medicine who did not give up on me and guided me into medical school
- My medical school classmates
- The General Conference of Seventh-day Adventists for accepting me and my family as missionaries
- The Ethiopian Union Mission for allowing me to serve
- The humanitarian aid agencies I labored with or had contact with while in Ethiopia: ADRA (The Adventist

Development and Relief Agency), CRDA (the Christian Relief and Development Association), Catholic Relief Services, USA for Africa, Africare, Oxfam, and the International Red Cross

- World Vision for their reports on US television that moved me to be a missionary
- The many expatriates I came to know, fellowship with, and collaborate with in Ethiopia
- Many Ethiopian citizens who were my colleagues in health ministry
- My co-workers at the Colorado Permanente Medical Group and Exempla Saint Joseph Hospital in Denver
- The many churches in the Denver metro area who allowed me to speak and be a part of their ministry
- The Body of Christ News and their publisher Mr. Randy McCowan who have allowed me to be a writer for them since 1995
- Humanitarian organizations in the Denver metro area doing community service and with whom my wife and I have collaborated: The Center for African American Health, the Colorado Black Health Collaborative, the American Diabetes Association, the Alzheimer's Association of Colorado, the Greater Denver Interfaith Alliance, the Inner City Health Center, the American Heart Association, and the Colorado Black Arts Festival.
- The North American Division of Seventh-day Adventists for allowing me to be an instructor for their annual health summit

Contents

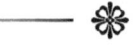

Prologue 13

Midnight Musing 17
Culture Shock 23
Anatomy of a Famine 33
Starvation: Kwashiorkor and Marasmus 43
Into the Crucible 51
Expired Medicine?-No Thanks! 91
A Near Death Experience 99
The State of The World's Children 105
Mission to America 117
Donor Fatigue 131

Bibliography 135

Prologue

"And there was a famine in the land…"
                                                    Genesis 12:10

I REMEMBER HIM AS I first saw him: gaunt, disheveled, and shivering violently after being caught in a rainstorm. He was nearly naked, and the tattered rags he was wearing revealed a body that was skeletal. His cheeks were deeply sunken and his eyes were blank and seemed focused on infinity. He did not seem to see those around him. In response to our questions, he remained mute. He had a family—his mother and sister were with him and amazingly they looked well fed. This adolescent looked as if he had passed the point of no return for a famine victim. (I had observed that when they were too thin and wasted, no amount of food and warm clothing would help, or change the inevitable outcome.) It was distressing to think that there in Makale, Ethiopia; there were legions more like him. I will call him Desta. As a missionary physician, I was duty bound to do something. I could not just watch him die.

We did what we could for Desta. We removed the vestiges of the rags he was wearing in full view of the workers on the clinic compound. We covered him with warm, albeit oversized clothing donated from America. A thick blanket became his overcoat.

However, he continued to shiver violently. A large bowl of porridge was brought to him, but to our amazement, he refused to eat, and no amount of coaxing would make him do otherwise. It appeared to me that death was soon to come for Desta. However, after some thought, I came to a creative alternative. We would take him to a "relief hospital" which was actually a group of tents. It was representative of the efforts of the many aid organizations working during the famine of 1984-1985 in Ethiopia in East Africa.

Using our mission's jeep as an ambulance, we took Desta to the tent hospital. I discussed his plight with the physician in charge although his predicament was obvious. I had to turn his care over to the physician and hope for the best. I prayed for his survival. I decided to come back two days later to see what had happened.

We returned to check on Desta. I walked into the tent hospital two days later and there was Desta sitting up in bed! He looked more alert and responsive. It was an answer to prayer. I asked the physician in charge what had happened, and he told me that they had inserted a feeding tube via the nostril into Desta's stomach. Desta had resisted at first, but the hospital nurses were persistent. Through the tube they had infused a liquid feeding. It was effective. Desta's appetite returned and now he was willing to eat whatever we gave him.

Desta returned to the care of my little clinic. We had a twice daily feeding program which involved feeding donated "high energy biscuits", and an oatmeal-like porridge. Desta came to our clinic daily to receive his food ration, along with about 100 other famine victims.

During the next month, we witnessed an astounding transformation in Desta. He changed from a living skeleton to a robust appearing adolescent. His cheeks and limbs filled out, and we could no longer see his ribs protruding. He thanked us profusely, and daily. We knew that if we had not taken him to the relief hospital, he would not have survived. He was truly a brand plucked out of the fire.

One day Desta and his family stopped coming to our clinic as many of those displaced by the famine returned to their villages. I never saw him again. However, to this day, his face haunts my memories. Strange as it may seem, I remember him mostly as I first saw him–a person on the verge of perishing. It is an experience God will not let me forget. It has been however, good to remember Desta's face, as it prevents me from becoming insensitive to the pain and suffering of those who dwell with me in my community, and on this planet.

Many years have passed since my term of service in Ethiopia. Despite this, memories keep flooding back. You may call them flashbacks. My life, the life of my wife and children would have been different had we not stayed the nearly three years we spent in Ethiopia. We learned much about ourselves and the country we served. After returning home to Colorado, my wife and I decided that we were still missionaries, but now to our own countrymen. In fact, working here in America, I imagined at times I was treating by proxy the people of Ethiopia. Once a missionary, always a missionary.

This book should have been written, and perhaps published years ago, but now is the time. The memories I have are compelling and enduring. I hope some good results from sharing these reflections.

I hope and pray to God that your understanding of what happened in Ethiopia and to my family will enlighten and inspire you. It is a call for action and compassion. We can't solve all of the world's pain and suffering, but we can try anyway!

Byron E. Conner MD

Midnight Musing

--- ✣ ---

"My heart was hot within me, while I was musing the fire burned: then spake I with my tongue."

Psalms 39:3

INTRACTABLE INSOMNIA LED ME and my family to a life-changing and unforgettable chapter in our lives. My wife, my two children and I were living in Visalia, California during my two-year stint as a physician with the US Public Health Service in nearby Earlimart, California. The term of service was nearly at an end. I was pondering what to do next as far as future medical practice was concerned. My insomnia became even worse while I was just considering just where we should go and what to do. During one of the many nights when sleep fled from me, I found myself sitting in front of the television set surfing the channels. Suddenly, pictures on the screen had my undivided and rapt attention. It was an informational fund-raising presentation by the aid organization World Vision presented in early 1984. It revealed that there was a famine in Ethiopia. Ethiopia, I thought. Just where was that? I learned it was a large portion of the "horn of Africa" in the northeastern region of the continent. I did not know much about that country at that time, but I was to learn more than I had ever known before.

The rains had failed, the drought produced food shortfalls in Ethiopia. Eight million people were at risk of being subjected to a devastating famine. The country was being run by a Marxist and it seemed to me a repressive government. I have to admit I was somewhat callous at first in considering this news. What could I do about the situation? As terrible as it seemed, what was happening had some overriding political overtones in my view. I did not see at first that the victims there were the powerless and the innocent.

Night after night with my family asleep, I sat and watched the same scenes replayed over and over. There before my eyes were wasted, emaciated children with their faces covered with flies and looking miserable beyond belief. The mothers of those children looked hopeless as they tried to breast feed their skeletal children. I became obsessed with watching those pictures. It was not merely a morbid fascination, but a growing feeling that someone should do something about this. Gradually, I started to feel that that "someone" should be me. I was nearing the end of my term of service on my job at the time, so I thought; perhaps I can go to Ethiopia to help out somehow.

Most importantly, I came to believe that it was God's will that I go to do something to help. In other words, I had a mission to perform. I did not know how to do it, but I had to do whatever I could. There were however other concerns. First of all, I had a wife and two children: my daughter Kellie who was 10 years old and my son Kevin who was 5 years of age. If I did go to Ethiopia, they would have to go with me. How was I going to support them if I became a missionary? Secondly, I had a plan to take a fellowship to become a specialist in taking care of cancer patients in the field of hematology/oncology. It seemed to me that if I did go to Africa as I was thinking, I was going to have to give up on the idea of entering the specialty I was considering.

I also did an introspective look back on my life. I thought about everything that happened to lead me to that point in my life. I relived many experiences and it seemed to me that overall, God had had a master plan for my life and I believed also a plan for the future.

I was born in Denver, Colorado. I was to be the oldest of 11 children of an obviously large family. I thought of the major milestones in my life. I joined the Seventh-day Adventist Church at the age of 9. I learned in the church the value of education and the notion that the education you received empowered you to serve. I attended a Seventh-day Adventist college in Lincoln, Nebraska: Union College from 1966 to 1968 and 1970 to 1972. I had been a premed student for a time, but an undisciplined one. In fact, one semester at Union in 1968 my grades were two F's, two D's and one C. I almost flunked out. As it turned out, I was to have a fateful encounter later on with a chemistry teacher named Dr. Rene Evard, who gave me one of the F's.

I served in the US Army from 1968-1970 including a tour in Vietnam. I returned to Union College from 1970-1972, majoring in sociology and then theology. I returned to Denver, Colorado and met my wife Alfredia, in our church parking lot! She was from San Bernardino, California. We moved to my wife's hometown and got married in 1973. We had discussed my finishing up a degree in theology and my becoming a church pastor. However, one month after our marriage I had a rather dramatic and sudden change of plans. I had a strong impression that the Lord was leading me to go into medicine. This was an unexpected change of plans as I had almost flunked out of college previously when I was a premed major at Union College! However, the idea of going into medicine became a powerful and persistent obsession, and I felt like it was something I was meant to do by God's grace.

I looked into the requirements for medical school and even went to visit nearby Loma Linda University, in Loma Linda California. I took an appointment with the dean of admissions which was at the time the late Dr. Rene Evard. This was the man who had given me the F in general chemistry at Union College!

At the appointed hour, the secretary had me walk into Dr. Evard's office and there he was sitting behind his desk. He took one look at me and I thought for a while he was going to faint! His mouth was wide open and he was speechless for a short time. Then he said to me: "I remember you!" I told Dr. Evard that I wanted to get into medical school. I admitted that in the past I had done poorly when I was a science major. Dr. Evard advised me to take again the courses I had done poorly in as well as all the other required courses. I attended subsequently San Bernardino Valley College and California State College at San Bernardino (now a university) majoring in Biology. My grades were much better, but I was not a straight A student. I was blessed however to score very well on the MCAT (Medical College Admission Test) which was required for medical school admission. I saw Dr. Evard after the MCAT test and he was quite pleased. He told me I should be "optimistic" about being accepted into medical school, and I was in fact accepted. Not long after our meeting, I received a letter stating: "Congratulations, you have been granted an acceptance to the Loma Linda University School of Medicine." The class was to matriculate in March 1976. It was to be essentially a three-year program without summers off.

The first half of our training was spent in learning the "basic sciences": anatomy, physiology, pharmacology, microbiology, and biochemistry. I had another encounter with Dr. Evard during the biochemistry course during the first year of medical school. He was to be our instructor in one section of our biochemistry course. I came to his first lecture and sat on the first row of the lecture hall and waited for the class to begin. Dr. Evard was standing in front of the classroom waiting for the class period to begin. He just stood there looking around the room. Our eyes met and he gave me a little smile. It was ironic and surreal that we would have an encounter like this now. The last time we had met, I received a failing grade in his class. I was determined to do well in his class now. As it turned out, when I took the required national standardized test of the basic sciences, biochemistry was my top score. This taught me not to just give up in the face of failure. I was grateful to God for the way things turned out. I am also grateful to this day for the support and encouragement I received from the late Dr. Evard.

I attended Loma Linda University School of Medicine from 1976-1979. Our two children were born in the medical center where

I trained. I was blessed in that I graduated in the upper third of my class. I subsequently did an arduous and hectic three-year residency in internal medicine in Denver at Saint Joseph Hospital from 1979 to 1982. After my training, we moved to Visalia, California to do 2 years of duty with the US Public Health Service to pay back the scholarship that had helped pay for my medical school expenses. I worked in a clinic that gave primary medical care to mostly farm workers in the San Joaquin Valley, many of them natives of Mexico, Central America, and the Philippines. In retrospect, this was good preparation for being in the mission field, as I learned the need to respect other cultures, and I learned the need to communicate despite language barriers.

I replayed in my mind repeatedly my life's history. I also thought about the powerful compulsion I was feeling to go to Ethiopia to help. I discussed things with my wife. She was supportive of my desire to go and my desire became her desire! However, I still had misgivings. My children were so young. We were going to travel so far away. Would I and my family be safe? What would happen after our stay in Ethiopia?

Meanwhile, the news reports from Ethiopia revealed an immense human tragedy like none that I had ever heard of before. I thought again about 8 million people being at risk for starvation. In addition, millions lived in abject poverty and in inhuman conditions. I was in a position to help. If I was going to go to help, it would have to be now. It seemed that the needs of the people I was going to serve were more important than all other considerations. I felt compelled to act. The future was uncertain, but I just prayed that I was making the right decision.

I contacted the headquarters of the Seventh-day Adventist church in Maryland, and told them essentially, we were at their service. We wanted to go to help out however we could in the crisis in Ethiopia. They were not calling me; I was calling them to offer my time and my efforts. After some discussion, I learned what the church expected of me. It was to be 6 years of service as a missionary, with a mid-term 3-month furlough. My job title was to be the Health and Temperance Director of the Ethiopian Union Mission. My job description was to be in charge of eight clinics and a rural hospital. I was also being asked to help set up something called a "Better Living Center" in the capital city Addis Ababa, and to conduct 5 Day Plans to Quit Smoking. I was a little uneasy with the fact that my brief job description did not really mention <u>anything</u> about famine relief. I just thought this was an oversight, or an out of date job description that did not fully describe what I would be doing. It was June of 1984. Prior to beginning our mission service, we would go to Andrew's University in Berrien Springs, Michigan for a one-month orientation, during July of 1984. This time of orientation was referred to as: "Mission Institute". We would subsequently have one month to visit our families in Denver, and California, and then we would be on our way to Ethiopia in August of 1984. We learned during our orientation program to expect the unexpected. My first desire on going abroad was to help those who needed help the most. I had no desire to have a job title, sit in an office, do some traveling and be an "administrator". I did indeed do these things, but an unexpected and fortuitous turn of events propelled me into a period of intense, and actually bittersweet service as a relief worker for famine victims. The latter was not in my job description, but this was the reason I had called the church to go for mission service. I did not and could not have foreseen some events that were to occur.

Amazingly, all of our plans and arrangements happened after my late nights in the throes of insomnia!

Culture Shock

--- ❦ ---

"Culture shock is the physical and emotional discomfort of being in a foreign country, another culture, an unfamiliar place, or all three."

USAID

ONCE MY WIFE AND I had decided that we would be missionaries, preparation was needed. This preparation included our young children: my daughter Kellie (ten years of age), and my son Kevin (5 years of age). We told our children where we were going and amazingly they had little to say about this. For them, it was just another move!

I had some second thoughts. I was concerned that I was going to put my family in danger. After all there was famine, disease, and warfare going on in Ethiopia. The country was very poor and I was concerned about the type of house we would live in, what we would eat, what type of medical care would be available, and what unknown threats and dangers awaited us. We prayed about the move and we were convinced we were doing the right thing. Our help was in fact needed in Ethiopia. There was hunger in the country, along with illness and a shortage of physicians. It did look like I was going to have to defer and perhaps give up my desire to become a specialist in hematology/oncology for sure at home in America, and more and more I had misgivings about this. However, it was not enough to change my plans to travel as planned.

I learned more and more about my expected duties

We discovered soon however, that I was to have some conflict with people who had authority over me in Ethiopia. My purported job description was that I was to be the "health and temperance director" for the Ethiopian Union Mission which included the countries of Ethiopia and neighboring Djibouti. (We had no facilities in Djibouti when I arrived). I was to be in charge of 8 clinics in various locations in the country, and a hospital in the town of Gimbie, far away in the western part of the country. What did I know about supervising a clinic or hospital in a foreign land, or at home? Nothing! I also received nothing to help me know how to oversee those facilities. In addition, I was to try to do "five-day" plans to help people quit smoking as this is what my predecessor had been doing as far as community outreach. (He was a pastor without medical training.) This smoking cessation program seemed incongruous to me in a country in the grip of high infant mortality, famine, disease, war and poverty. Finally, I was charged with creating a facility called a "Better Living Center", in the capital city Addis Ababa which was to be a place to do health education seminars for people in the city. This would have appealed perhaps to the urban elite and would have been a nice "PR" gesture on the part of the church there in Addis Ababa.

I was to have the duty of sitting on the executive committee of the "Ethiopian Union Mission" of our church as a department head and administrator. Talk about culture shock! I had only wanted to come to Ethiopia to help famine victims and I was faced with all of the duties I just described. What this meant is that there was a fundamental disagreement between myself and my superiors. However, this disagreement was not open and blatant. I was thinking about starving children while I sat in committee meetings that did far too little, in my view, to help those children, and I was expected to do things that were inappropriate given the dire emergency in the country. I was dismayed and infuriated. Nevertheless, I tried to do what I could and play the hand I was dealt. I may have really had second thoughts about going to Ethiopia if I had known about all of the circumstances I would find. As it turned out however, I was in fact able to do some significant things to help those I really came to help, and I will always be grateful for that. In retrospect, I erred in not revealing to all concerned about my true reason for wanting to come to Ethiopia!

There is considerable time for other personal reflections and observations on a long trip to your final destination. Following farewells to our families and travel arrangements by our church, we found ourselves on a tiring trip to Ethiopia. We flew via Lufthansa Airlines from Los Angeles, California to Frankfort, Germany for the first leg of our journey. It was a non-stop 10-hour ride. I thought frequently during the trip about what we would find after arriving at our destination. I wondered if I had made the right decision. I had felt compelled to do what we are doing, but intermittently I had second thoughts. Perhaps I should have just done the fellowship in hematology/oncology I had had a passion to do it. I was grateful that I had survived and in fact thrived in medical school, had endured an arduous residency in internal medicine, and for the two years after residency had served in the US Public Health Service in Earlimart, California. I was grateful that I had an extremely supportive wife, and tolerant children. I watched them as we flew and they tolerated the trip well, doing mostly sleeping. The jet was a large 747 with two aisles and plenty of room. We were well fed so much so, that I marveled and I wondered where they were storing so much food.

We landed in Frankfort, Germany after our ten-hour trip. I had had thoughts of seeing Frankfort, the city as we had a 24 hour layover. However, our jet lag did not permit us to do this, and we spent the bulk of the time before the next leg of our journey sleeping.

The next phase of our journey was from Frankfort, Germany to Jeddah, Saudi Arabia. We did not deplane and were on the ground just a short time. Then we were set to land in Addis Ababa, in Ethiopia. The name Addis Ababa meant "new flower". We arrived after night fall, on a Thursday evening, August, 1984. As the door to the aircraft opened and we descended the mobile staircase, and we were greeted by the pungent odor of a new land and a new part of the world. It seemed surreal that we were now on the other side of the world. We were greeted by a fellow American missionary, who was a pastor, and mission department head, and I was grateful for his warm and enthusiastic greeting.

We traveled by car from Bole International Airport to our place of residence on a fenced church compound referred to as "kabana". On the compound with us were a small church, a school, and a printing house which published church literature in Amharic. The American pastor gave us a running commentary and orientation to the city. We drove along the streets of a modern looking city as near as we could tell. We drove past many office buildings, hotels and foreign embassies. Our compound was behind Menelek II Hospital which was operated by the Ethiopian Ministry of Health. We were to find ourselves in a comfortable modern house with many of the comforts of home, and we were grateful for this.

Addis Ababa was actually a city I came to love. It was a big sprawling city of over 1 million in 1984. It is a high-altitude capital with an elevation about 7,700 feet as I was informed and was even higher than my native Denver. The high altitude allowed us to escape the risk of malaria. The climate was awesome with an average high in the 70-degree F. range. We had arrived during the end of the rainy season, but I loved the daily brief rainfall. I loved the green rolling hills. The city was a mixture of modern buildings, and many mud houses in which the urban poor resided.

I was grateful that we were to live in a comfortable home that exceeded my expectations. I was going to have to do some traveling and I was thinking, at least my wife and children would be in a comfortable place. We even were able to shop and eat our usual vegetarian diet which we had consumed at home. There was a good variety of food and plenty of it which seemed surprising in a country in the grip of a devastating famine.

The following morning, we all were taken by our pastor guide to the Ethiopian Union Mission office which was near the center of town. It was quite striking to see the juxtaposition of the old and new. There were small herds of goats, cattle and sheep in the streets, and drivers had to weave their way around these. Near the center of town there were soldiers standing on the streets holding AK47s, needless to say an intimidating sight, but they were actually non-threatening to us.

The compound for the Ethiopian Union Mission included a large church, and an office building. I was introduced to the workers on the compound and the Union officials who seemed cordial enough. I had my own separate office. There was in the office building a large committee room where I was to spend too many hours in my view sitting in committee meetings. This setup was not what I had envisioned in my thoughts of coming to Ethiopia to serve victims of the famine. I was really going to be an administrator, not my concept of being a missionary.

I was able to spend some time walking the streets of Addis Ababa around the mission compound. It gave me more of a perspective to add to what I could see driving around. There were modern hotels and restaurants near the compound which served western style food. There were beggars on the streets of Addis Ababa and they readily approached foreigners. They could quickly tell I was not a native despite the fact that the hue of my skin was like theirs. They would just hold out their hands and make what sounded like a hissing noise. I saw some beggars who were maimed and had been the victims of polio as I surmised. These individuals were actually crawling on the ground dragging their withered legs and with their hands inside a pair of shoes.

Near the church compound was the Black Lion Hospital which was a huge teaching hospital for the country's medical school. There were offices for the United Nations, and the World Health

Organization. Scattered around the center of town were signs that said: "Long Live Marxism-Leninism" and others that said: "COPWE's Mission Shall Be Fulfilled!" COPWE was a committee that was working to organize the Worker's Party of Ethiopia which meant essentially a one-party Marxist government. There were a number of embassies near the center of town, and it made for a fascinating urban arrangement.

The Marxist government seemed oppressive. The soldiers in the streets, and the obvious censorship of books and newspapers affected even foreigners. There were significant travel restrictions and one had to obtain permission to travel outside Addis Ababa unless it was a relatively short trip. We even had a worker tasked with going to a government office to get travel documents for us expatriates to visit different parts of the country. I had to travel to visit the medical facilities we had in the country in my task as the Health and Temperance Director. You did not dare travel to a place without travel documents as required.

I felt sympathetic with the Ethiopian natives as they did in fact live in a repressive regime. We had arrived 10 years after a Marxist coup had over- thrown Emperor Haile Selassie. The country was ruled be an Ethiopian despot Mengistu Haile Mariam. This ruler had reigned with brutality. He had a political system with kept close surveillance it seemed over everyone. The people who lived in Addis Ababa were part of kebeles, (which were also in the rural area) or a so-called urban dwellers association which included about 3,000 to 12,000 people. The head of this kebele could be a small dictator himself and I learned of situations where the kebele head had jailed people. We expatriates learned to live and function in the political atmosphere as it existed then.

The day we arrived at our new residence in Addis Ababa, my young 5-year-old son was really impressed that we were now in Africa. He kept saying repeatedly: "I can't believe we are in Africa!" My son and daughter adapted rapidly to our new country. Their only complaint came from my daughter who though the locals stared at us too much when we were out and about around town. It was obvious to me that the locals knew we were not Ethiopians and perhaps they stared at us to figure out where we were from. My son quickly picked up Amharic, which was along with English an official language. There were actually about 80 languages in the country. My wife and I had not had formal language studies as we had thought we would have and we were far less proficient in learning Amharic. As it turned out many people spoke English and in fact the instruction in schools across the country was often in English.

We had arrived on a Thursday evening in August 1984. I received a surprise on Friday evening when someone came to our house, greeted us cordially, and then informed me that I would be preaching the sermon on Saturday morning in the small Seventh-day Adventist Church there on the compound. I then spent a good part of the night preparing for this. I spoke the next day on the subject: "Where is Your True Home?" The thrust of my sermon was that we are all just passing through this world and our true home was in heaven. This was a good initiation for me as I was to preach many sermons there, including in the largest Seventh-day Adventist church in Addis Ababa. When one preached a translator stood next to you. You spoke a sentence or clause in English and this was translated into the major language Amharic by the translator. (Although English was also taught in the schools) That meant your message had to be relatively brief.

In our home we entertained many of the visitors who came to Addis Ababa from abroad and had business at the Ethiopian Union Mission. My wife became quite proficient at preparing awesome meals for our guests. Also, we had an Ethiopian helper, a young lady who assisted my wife in preparing food and house cleaning. We also had Ethiopian dishes which consisted of *injera*-the local equivalent of bread which was flat with a spongy texture, eaten with *wat*. This *wat* was various vegetable stews, and for people who ate meat there was a *wat* made with meat such as chicken. The *wat* was seasoned with a hot reddish spice called *beriberi*. You ate with your hands. I developed a real taste for Ethiopian food as long as it is vegetarian. I still love it too this day.

There was a large expatriate community in Addis Ababa. Given the many NGOs (non-governmental organizations with a humanitarian focus), churches, international health agencies and foreign embassies, there was a true international group in Ethiopia. We got to know and meet people from every part of the globe. To this day, I have friends who were living and working in Ethiopia along with their families. There were a number of missionaries both within and outside of my church who we spent considerable time with. Some of us are still friends and keep in touch to this day.

From time to time representatives of the various NGOs assembled to meet with the Ethiopian Relief and Rehabilitation Committee. We received briefings about the needs of the country in terms of famine relief from the person in charge of the government entity at that time-Comrade Dawit. There were also unofficial channels of communication which were surprisingly accurate but not approved by the government. All of us expatriates were aware of proper precautions and protocols to live and work in an authoritarian regime and be there to help the millions at risk. At times we disagreed with the government's policies and practices, but we did not openly contest things.

From time to time my wife and I and our children visited the American Embassy in Addis Ababa. In fact, my wife worked there briefly as a teacher. We attended a briefing there at the embassy and we heard a report from an American economist. She told us that in 1984 and as she spoke, that Ethiopia was the poorest country in the world. It did not seem so apparent living in Addis Ababa as the government tried as much as possible to create as rosy picture as possible. However, those of us who traveled to the countryside knew better.

Our children were blessed to be able to attend a school for expatriate children called Bingham Academy. The teachers were often from the US, and my son had a teacher from Australia. The students were from America, Europe, Asia, South America, and other African countries. The importance of our children's education was one reason why we did not stay in Ethiopia as long as we should have as the school only went to the eighth grade.

One of the most shocking things we witnessed shortly after arriving in Ethiopia was an unbelievable celebration that took place in Ethiopia. One night on September 10th, the skies over Addis Ababa were filled with of all things-fireworks. The display of pyrotechnics was to celebrate the 10th year of the revolution that overthrew Emperor Haile Selassie. It seemed almost obscene to see such a display for the poorest country in the world in the grip of famine, disease and internal warfare. It made me more determined to try to understand the reasons for the famine of 1984, and to just reinforce and focus my passion for being in Ethiopia.

Anatomy of a Famine

---- ❊ ----

"Man can and must prevent the tragedy of famine in the future instead of merely trying with pious regret to salvage the human wreckage of the famine, as he has so often done in the past."

Norman Borlaug

THE ETHIOPIAN FAMINE OF 1984-1985 was an event that caused a robust response from a multitude of people in the world community. "Let us include the time frame of the 1980's for the famine and the humanitarian crisis." I am one of those people who was stimulated to act. I did not have to, but I felt compelled to do so. Why should I and others do something to help people on the other side of the globe? After all, the vast majority of those of us motivated to help the famine victim would never see or touch those victims. However, the video presentations taken by news organizations such as the BBC, and others found their way into our living rooms. The world community was moved to act.

I eventually saw many of those famine victims, up close and personal. I even learned the names of some of them. In this book, there are pictures I took that will allow you to see some of their faces. As I looked at them, I asked myself why was this happening to them? I learned that there was an unfortunate mix of circumstances: geopolitical forces, capricious weather changes, inertia, poverty, internal intrigue, and disease which served to cause immense suffering and death. There was and is plenty of blame to go around.

Many in the world came to Ethiopia to help. They came from the democratic countries of the West as well as from countries in the socialist realm. About 1 billion dollars poured into the country to assist. Money was raised by concerts, and musicians with hit singles such as: "We are the World", and "Do They Know It's Christmas?" Aid organizations such as the one who caught my eye-World Vision-had televised reports that compelled us to act. I applaud all of those who helped in any way they could. Many lives were saved I am sure, by Ethiopians and many in the international community.

I learned from multiple sources reasons for the suffering in Ethiopia. The aid workers I collaborated with were a source of information at times albeit clandestine due to the censorship in the country. The Ethiopian government through the Relief and Rehabilitation Commission would brief aid organizations about the needs of the country. I observed some things with my own eyes. Some of what I have learned has been now in retrospect from historical sources. Some of the explanations for the famine have to do with preexisting conditions that had existed for decades prior to the famine of 1984-1985. This confluence of situations together produced a burden of suffering that continues to this day.

In the field of internal medicine when rendering care to patients we create what we call a "problem list". This is a snapshot of the health issues a patient may have. Often the set of problems may be complex with some interactions between problems that make for a challenging state of affairs. However, this problem list allows for efficacious and appropriate action. Based on this concept, here is my problem list for Ethiopia *in the context of the famine of 1984-1985*. (Note that the items listed are not necessarily in order of importance, as all are important, and some information is from the expatriate network.)

My Problem List for Ethiopia

1) <u>A Repressive Marxist Government with a history of violence</u>: It was an intimidating experience to arrive on the scene in Addis Ababa and see some of the streets lined with soldiers armed with automatic weapons. I learned that there was unyielding censorship of the written and broadcast word and expatriates also had to be careful about the words that came out of their mouths, even if facts were correct. There were strict travel restrictions and it was necessary for us expatriates to make an application and receive permission to travel in the country except for short distances near Addis Ababa. At times we felt like our hands were tied when we wanted to go to certain places to help people. To be fair, I am sure that those in the government had to also feel intimidated with the flood of expatriates from multiple countries and those people came with political thinking inimical to Marxism-Leninism.

   My wife, children and I arrived in the country 10 years after the military revolution that overthrew the monarch Haile Selassie who had ruled Ethiopia since 1930. Oddly enough a famine was a factor that lead in part to his being deposed. There was a famine in the early 1970's in Welo and Tigray provinces in which about 200,000 people died. The monarch allegedly concealed the famine. There were also concerns with land reform, economics and corruption. Civilian and military unrest lead to the arrest and to the monarch being deposed September 12, 1974. Haile Selassie died the following year in detention and was secretly buried. There was a group of military personnel who came to rule the country in the midst of maneuvering and much bloodshed. Emerging out of this turmoil was a committee: The Provisional Military Administrative Council. (Also referred to as the Derg-Amharic for committee) The chairman of the Derg was Major Mengistu Haile Mariam, who came to be the ruler of Ethiopia.

It was unfortunate that the Derg and "Comrade Mengistu" were unable to lead Ethiopia down a pathway of progress. Instead, the Derg was ruling the country during one of the worst famines known. 600,000 deaths are estimated to have occurred on their watch. It was regrettable to see this happen, and I felt much sympathy for the people of Ethiopia.

2) <u>Internal and Regional Warfare</u>: Warfare swirled around Ethiopia. The country had been at war with Somalia (its eastern neighbor) over a tract of land between them called the Ogaden. Somalia had desired to annex this territory. Ethiopia had turned to the Soviet Union for assistance which supplied military aid. Cuban troops also aided Ethiopia, and Somalian forces were driven back across the border and defeated in 1978. There was involved in this conflict an insurgent group: the Western Somali Liberation Front which had collaborated with the Somali National Army.

There were other insurgent groups active in Ethiopia including: the Eritrean Liberation Front (ELF), the Eritrean People's Liberation front (EPLF), the Tigray People's Liberation Front (TPLF), and the Oromo Liberation Front (OLF). These groups made helping the citizens of Ethiopia far more hazardous as they engaged in warfare with the Ethiopian army. Imagine trying to supply famine relief in areas of such conflict. I was never aware of any direct armed conflict that I could witness or even hear of during my stay in the northern part of Ethiopia. I just know that the only way I could travel between Addis Ababa and Makale was by air: first the Royal Air Force of Britain, then later by commercial flights with Ethiopian Airlines.

Eventually insurgents of the ELF, EPLF and TPLF defeated Mengistu's forces in the provinces of Eritrea and Tigray and by 1988 controlled most of that territory. Eventually, Eritrea the northern most portion of Ethiopia, became a new independent country in 1993, leaving the balance of the country as a landlocked nation. This followed a 30-year war for independence.

I understood the conflicts raging during my time in Ethiopia, but I could not, and did not concern myself much with that. I was too occupied trying to take care of the many coming to my clinic for assistance

3) <u>Drought, Crop Failure, Economic Collapse</u>: My earliest memory of the famine and the humanitarian crisis in Ethiopia included the reports of the drought and crop failure. This we can be sure, also included loss of livestock, the ability to earn income, and starvation for the numerous subsistence farmers and their families. Just imagine what it would be like if you lost your job, your source of food, and even had the demise of family members. There was no such thing as insurance, social services, unemployment benefits or anyone to turn to. Your neighbors, and the members of your extended family were in the same circumstances. There was no one to turn to. You ended up then leaving your homestead to any place you could turn to for help. I assumed when I saw the multitude of displaced people I saw that they were enduring the scenario described and ended up in the relief camp I saw in Makale in Northern Ethiopia. There were similar camps I heard about at Korem and Alamata.

It seems less dehumanizing and demeaning when you pause to think about what displaced people are going through. We should not see them as just faceless, unnamed people. The sheer number of people seeking help made seeing them as individuals a significant challenge. Perhaps however, if we see them as individuals who needs help, we might be more zealous and compassionate in our attempts to help despite feeling overwhelmed.

During 1984-1987 (the time of my stay in Ethiopia) we can note that drought was not new to Ethiopia. There had been recurrent famine since the early 1970's. For years, hunger was a frequent specter for Ethiopia and states in the Sahel: Senegal, Mauritania, Mali, Burkina Faso, Niger, Chad, and Sudan. Drought is inimical to adequate food production. Given crop failure, warfare, and economic collapse, there is a recipe to produce a substantial misery level.

Farmers in Ethiopia produce crops such as coffee, corn, sorghum, wheat, millet, barley, and teff (an indigenous crop used to make Ethiopian bread called *injera*). In part, the poverty of the country may be related to the fact that the chief cash crop was coffee. This was not to my mind a commodity that would bring a robust foreign exchange income. Coffee is obviously a crop subject to volatility in terms of profit and revenue.

4) <u>Resettlement and Villagization</u>: In response to the famine, the ruling entity in Ethiopia, the Derg carried out the unpopular and much criticized schemes that included the involuntary movement of large masses of the peasants. In resettlement, peasants were often forcibly moved from the worst famine affected areas of the north to the south and southwest in Ethiopia. It is estimated that in 1985 and 1986, 600,000 people were moved. Family members were separated, and it was noted that thousands perished during and after the transfer of people.

Villagization involved a system to require peasants to live in government mandated clusters of designated villages that were to facilitate the delivery of needed services. Citizens were hypothetically to receive water supply, schools, electricity, and medical care in these crafted villages. It turned out that the government was unable to provide the needed services, and the people reacted negatively to the scheme.

It was charged by the international community that resettlement and villagization were in part ploys to combat the insurgent forces in Eritrea and Tigray by reducing the population base. The expatriate discussion and belief were that these tactics simply did not help the humanitarian crisis in the country. Agricultural productivity actually dropped, and peasants resorted to simply fleeing the country, and also once relocated tried to make their way back home. It just added to our belief that the government was not willing or capable of coping in a reasonable manner with the calamity in Ethiopia.

5) <u>Displaced People and Refugees</u>: There was an unfortunate and chaotic movement of people within Ethiopia and to and from neighboring countries. By definition refugees are those who flee the confines of their own country for another land. Displaced people move within their own country to a different region. I became well acquainted with those displaced by the famine as they were those who came to live in the large tents and temporary barn-like buildings near my clinic in Makale in Tigray province. They had to abandon their homes or perish. Ethiopians fled also to neighboring countries: Sudan, Somalia, Kenya, and Djibouti. In addition, there were citizens of Sudan who fled to Ethiopia because of conflict between the Sudanese government and the Sudanese Liberation Army (SPLA). Citizens of Somalia fled to Ethiopia because of conflict between the government of Somalia and the Somali National Movement (SNM). The observation was noted that the refugee situation in the Horn of Africa about the time of the mid-1980s was the worst on the planet with about 2.5 million people fleeing their homeland for another country.

I tried to wrap my mind around what it would be like to be a refugee due to abuse, warfare, repression, famine, and death. What were these people going to find in the place they fled to? They would find a life of squalor in a refugee camp, and likely abuse from some who attended the camp. Their hunger would not end. They would be at risk of contracting a communicable disease due to the congestion in the camps. I think it is safe to say that we would be hard pressed to find more miserable people on this globe we live on. What really disturbed me is that I was powerless to change this situation although I certainly wanted to.

6) <u>Insufficient Medical Care</u>: From my standpoint, the Ethiopian government medical care system for the most part reflected the poverty of the country. There just seemed to be a lack of everything. It was a momentous adjustment for me to work in the health arena in Ethiopia after spending 5 years as a physician training and practicing in the US. I had gotten accustomed to well supplied clinics and hospitals with a full array of services such as laboratory services, radiology, pharmacies, surgical suites well trained nurses, multiple specialists and many fellow internists. Budgets for hospitals and some clinics were in the multimillion dollar range. I realized after I arrived on the scene how much I had taken for granted working in the medical care system in the US. In Ethiopia, I was shocked and appalled by what I found. I know now that in 1983-1984 there were about 546 physicians present in the country to serve a population of 42 million people. This meant there was a ratio of 1 physician for every 77,000 people. Physicians indeed seemed hard to find. Specialists like the ones I was used to collaborating with back home were non-existent.

The hospitals I visited seemed devoid of supplies. I observed family members actually giving nursing care to their loved ones who were in the hospital. The clinic and hospital workers did labor valiantly to do their work. There seemed to be shockingly few options as far as available medications were concerned. This was in the city. In the rural areas, there was a paucity of medical care in scattered remote clinics which required at times walking for unacceptable distances for any type of medical care. The budget allotted for medical care was a fraction of that spent on the armed forces. This was especially true with the internal warfare going on.

I learned to work in the medical environment I found myself in. I was thankful that I was able to receive generous medication supplies sent from abroad to help me take care of my patients. I also learned to read everything I could get my hands on to give appropriate medical care to those who came my way.

The most serious health issues we had to deal with were malnutrition and infectious diseases. In Ethiopia, there are a large number of endemic infections that can infect indigenous people and expatriates alike. The names of these organisms may not be familiar to expatriates: Shistosomiasis, leishmaniasis, ascaris lubricoides, hookworm, trichuris trichuria were some of the parasitic worms encountered. There were other infections perhaps better known such as malaria, tuberculosis, measles, leprosy, tetanus, and meningococcal meningitis. Because of unsanitary conditions, crowding and just a suppressed immune system due to undernutrition we saw diarrhea, dysentery, pneumonia, skin infections, eye infections, and fever of unknown cause. The problem for me was that I just did not have lab facilities to make a precise diagnosis of what infection my patients had. In fact, they might have multiple infections in addition to being malnourished. We had to treat what we could see and that often meant treating diarrhea, pneumonia, skin and eye infections as often those were obvious. It was gratifying to see that patients did get better with simple treatment of things that were obvious even though I could not diagnose everything. What they needed most was better nutrition.

I do not mean to imply that the poor medical infrastructure was a cause of the famine. Instead I can say that the state of medical care just exacerbated the misery level. Despite this, I consider it an honor to have been there to try to help. I realize our own medical system in America is not perfect.

This is how I saw things in Ethiopia while I lived there. My conclusions of the major factors that caused or exacerbated the dreadful famine that struck Ethiopia are as noted. I was dismayed that I as an individual I could do so little to change the political, social, economic and health situation. I just had to be persistent in whatever I could do to assist. I am thankful that I was privileged to be there to do what I could do to help.

Starvation: Kwashiorkor and Marasmus

"By showing hunger, deprivation, starvation and brutality, as well as endurance and nobility, documentaries inform, prod our memories, even stir us to action. Such films do battle for our very soul."

Theodore Bikel

It is true that in America, we have the homeless, the destitute and the poverty stricken. However, on the whole we do not see any signs of mass starvation. Instead we have the perhaps unexpected conditions of our time which are overweight and obesity. We are talking about two-thirds of our country who tip the scale on the corpulent side. We use terms such as "plus sized". "king sized" and "queen sized", to describe our body habitus. We may decide to be charitable and describe an overweight person as "heavy" It is significant that obesity is common in our country even among the poor. We eat too much high calorie foods at times in gargantuan portions, and exercise too little. Many of us have struggled to lose weight at one time or another in America.

Working in the field of internal medicine, one can see that issues of body weight are noted constantly. Concomitant with this we see associated diseases such as heart disease, high blood pressure, diabetes, stroke and even cancer. I wish I could have received a special compensation every time I told a patient to lose weight in the various clinics in America that I worked in. After all of this, I was conditioned to see numerous patients who I exhorted to lose weight. It was often an exercise in futility.

Rarely, I did see in America unfortunate patients who had perhaps a terminal illness such as cancer who did in fact look as if they were starving. Their bodies were cachectic and wasted. However, this was rare. My mind was thus conditioned to think large as far as patients were concerned. It was therefore stunning to be in a situation where I saw a seemingly endless display of people who essentially looked terminal, and almost all of these were children. I was first struck by the utter powerlessness of those children. They did not ask for their plight and were totally at the mercy of their circumstances. In a famine and in other natural disasters, it just seems intuitively obvious that the most vulnerable individuals in the populace will suffer most. In fact, looking at the health status of children is a barometer of the state of affairs of a country. It was a bit overwhelming in addition to note that the number of cachectic children was immense in my view.

One of the first thoughts that came to my mind when I looked at those children who were obviously starving was who is responsible for this? Was it the parents? Was it the government of Ethiopia? Was it the international community? I was not the only person there to help but I wanted to help everyone, but I could not. I could not make it possible for every emaciated child I saw to get well and look as healthy as my own infant children had looked. There were just too many people besieging the medical facilities I did visit.

Along with everyone there to help, and that included Ethiopians and expatriates alike, there had to be a plan of action. We have all heard about and perhaps experienced "on the job training". It may at times seem like being thrown into the deep end of the pool and having to sink or swim. That was my experience. I had not been trained prior to coming to Ethiopia specifically how to care for starving children, or adults. However, I had to tend to those famished youngsters, and their elders coming to the clinic I eventually ran (as noted later). I did not need to provide just food, but also clothing, blankets, and as needed medication. The needs seemed overwhelming and that was to be expected with estimates of 8 million people facing starvation. This was in the midst of warfare, drought, crop and livestock losses, a poor infrastructure, poverty, and infectious disease.

We medical people just have to have a nomenclature and a clinical description for the things we are likely to treat. We have names for starvation: marasmus, and its cousin kwashiorkor. Both of these are manifestations of severe acute malnutrition or acute lack of nutrition adequate for good health and growth. We usually thought of children when using these terms. Marasmus is also described as severe wasting with an unbelievably skeletal child who appears moribund. In kwashiorkor one sees also an ill child who may not appear as ill as he or she really is. This is because the child has significant swelling of both feet and legs, and at times all over. The hair may be thin and may change color to a yellow or reddish hue. These are high risk children who may be 9 times more likely to die than well fed children. Almost all of the children I saw had marasmus.

Malnourished children can be said to have a catastrophic illness just like people in our own country who have strokes, heart attacks or severe trauma. These kids are at risk for dying and dying quickly. They lack things we take for granted like adequate protein, calories and essential nutrients. Along with the lack of food, there is a lack of vitamins and minerals. There will be deficiencies of vitamin A, folic acid, iron, zinc, copper, and perhaps we do not know the full impact of this undernourishment. It was obvious to me that the impact was devastating. Those children I saw were often dehydrated, and at risk for infections such as diarrhea, pneumonia and measles. They had suppressed immune systems and decreased ability to fight off infections. Too many children just expired suddenly on our clinic compound and I think they died of hypoglycemia (low blood sugar), hypothermia, (low body temperature), dehydration, and electrolyte imbalances. I could only use my eyes, and hands to make a diagnosis. One thing I did know is that if a child was too thin and wasted that the probability of death was very high. We still were unrelenting to do what we could in our clinic as did all of the NGOs working in the country. We were just dismayed at the sheer number of affected children. We did save some, but unfortunately, not all.

Among humankind today we have the haves, the have-nots and even those in between. In our own country, even if we have limited means, we can gorge ourselves to the point of being uncomfortably full, and too often that is exactly what we do. It would not change our eating habits perhaps, but we need to be aware of the fact that hunger affects up to one billion people on earth at any one time. Fifty-five million children are affected by acute malnutrition at this time and 6 million children die of hunger each year. For those children who do survive acute malnutrition, there are untold numbers who may have permanent changes in how they grow and they may have cognitive impairment. This tragedy is ongoing despite the fact we may not be cognizant of it. I don't have the solution to this problem and I am not sure any concerted effort can make it go away completely. However, we can do all we can do as there are those who work in needy places to bring help and comfort.

Even though it may seem like a daunting task, there are strategies and guidelines to instruct those working in the midst of catastrophic famine and hunger situations. These efforts take collaboration between NGOs and local and international governments. The efforts also take willing expatriates that will travel to a far-off place to work in concert with local people in the midst of poverty, disease, warfare, natural calamities, and distressing sights of misery.

So how do you feed a famine victim? The answer is carefully! It takes some thought and planning so as many lives as possible can be saved. We could not feed our parents their usual fare as that was simply not feasible or effective given the large number of victims. We had to have food that could be shipped easily, distributed efficiently, and be efficacious in relieving the severe malnutrition as much as possible. We had to feed those starving youngsters and their parents food that we could prepare and also place in their hands. We received in my clinic, 25-pound burlap bags of a grain mixture of wheat, corn, and soya flour. This mixture could be cooked into a gruel that reminded me of oatmeal that we could feed to people in a bowl. We washed the bowls in my experience and reused them. This was called a "wet ration". It was an effective and reasonable way to feed our patients and this was a common way to feed famine victims. Another food source we used was "high energy biscuits" which came in a packet and contained about 6 wafers about the size of graham crackers we eat here in America. This was also called a "dry ration" which could be carried away from the clinic.

If an NGO had the means, there were other things to do. First of all, children could be weighed, and we did do this. Another measurement that could be done was the height, and the mid-upper arm circumference. Inspection by just looking at a child told a lot as we could easily see the advanced wasting, which is what I frequently saw. We did in fact in the strategy of triaging, give food to those who needed it worse which were malnourished children and their breast-feeding mothers. The measured parameters could be monitored to see if a child was making progress. Blankets and clothing saved kids from hypothermia.

My clinic was not able to do it, but some organizations did "inpatient" treatment of famine victims giving frequent semi-liquid feedings, IV fluids, injectable antibiotics, oral antibiotics vitamin supplements, lab testing, and nurses to attend people. I was not able to have a place for patients in beds, but I did do as many of the other things as possible in an "outpatient" setting. I did see some gratifying improvement. It just required that I be resourceful in my treatment. However, as I took care of those malnourished children, I was thinking that back home such kids would be in a first-rate hospital and more than likely an intensive care unit. We did not have anything near such a luxury.

Think for a moment about the times you may have heard about a country in the midst of some natural calamity, or war. There may be a food emergency with an estimate given about the number that are facing starvation and the amount of food needed to avert mass casualties. In such a situation, you can be certain that many children have already died or been damaged by malnutrition, by the time the report is even given. After the food aid arrives, there are many challenges in delivering the food to those in need. It is essentially like trying to treat a desperately ill patient with advanced disease, except there are many such patients, and challenges in getting the food where it needs to be. The efforts are worth it. However, at times if you are a worker in the situation you will also wishing you had control over the political, social, health, and economic situation. However, that will not be the case. Therefore, you do the best you can and pray and hope for the best outcome. That is what I learned to do.

As an expatriate working in Ethiopia at the time I was there, besides the rampant hunger, there were other troubling things to contend with and to think about. There was the specter of infectious diseases such as malaria, tuberculosis, measles, cholera, and parasitic infections etc. (Fortunately, HIV/AIDS had not yet taken a foothold in Ethiopia, at least not as had been brought to my attention, or that of the medical community there). These infections just served to increase the mortality for vulnerable famine victims. The most frequent infections I saw were diarrhea, pneumonia, eye infections and skin infections. There was the distressing poverty, difficult travel and the oppressive nature of living in the confines of a Marxist regime.

A person dying of hunger is an event that should not happen in a world with the resources we have. Ethiopia is a beautiful country with beautiful people that was and is caught in a maelstrom of suffering.

I learned a lot about how to feed the hungry and often sick people I came in contact with. I learned from my reading, talking to other expatriates, and my own experience. It was gratifying to see and know that we were actually saving lives.

Taking care of starving citizens be they adults or children, has a soul-searing impact. It is something that has an indelible and unforgettable impact. Most of us working in a country where we are unlikely to see such patients have to go through a time of adjustment and a rapid education. There are fortunately sources of information and experienced people to help you. One thing that no one seems to mention and not intentionally, is that you will never be the same after caring for such people. You will forever experience a higher degree of compassion and concern that you may not have thought about for any future group of sick people no matter where they may be. You will also have memories that you will have as long as you live. This will serve you well and make you a better provider.

INTO THE CRUCIBLE

"Beloved, think it not strange concerning the fiery trial which is to try you, as though some strange thing happened unto you."

I Peter 4:12

IN 1984 AND 1985, the famine in Ethiopia was a maelstrom that was consuming people by the hundreds daily. There were some hotspots that I was aware of in Tigray province, in the northern portion of the country: the towns of Korem, Alamata, and Makale. At these places desperate peasants had congregated looking for food and respite. Large and temporary camps had been set up to care for these people. They were in fact places where people could be helped, but the misery that could be seen there was heartrending and unforgettable. The displaced and for the time homeless people were housed in large tent cities, and large barn-like structures. They were fed as possible donated food and at least they had some shelter. Families huddled together in wretchedness.

Makale (also designated Mekele, or Mekelle) was to be the focus of my attention and a place that has left an indelible mark on my psyche. I first went to Makale to inspect the work that was going on there. My church, (the Seventh-day Adventist church) had had a clinic operating there for years with a succession of missionary nurses serving there. The nurse who was there, was from the Philippines, and at that time was nearing the end of her term of service. I wanted to just go and have a look of things. There was no replacement yet for her. I went to spend 2 days in Makale.

To get to Makale I first had to get travel permission from the government. Makale, in Tigray province, was about 473 miles north of Addis Ababa where my family and I were living. Due to the terrain and the war going on between the central government and the Tigray People's Liberation Front, travel to Makale was to be done only by air. I would travel this time, and on some later trips with the British Air Force that was also flying in relief supplies. Arrangements were made, and I was allowed on the flight to Makale onboard a military aircraft, a C130. My enduring memory of those flights was excruciating nausea from the moment the plane left the ground until we touched down on the dirt landing strip in Makale.

The airplane flew over rugged mountains and plateaus. I could see remote villages and around them a green patchwork of cultivated areas that belied the devastating famine besieging the country. I arrived in Makale in September of 1984 for the planned 2-day visit. I was picked up at the airport and taken to the clinic. As we traveled to the clinic, I noticed a small-town ambience. There were some paved streets and a cluster of government buildings some of which looked like castles. Makale Adventist Clinic was a short walking distance from the center of town and the shopping district. The hotel in which I was to stay was up a hill from the clinic. The clinic nurse gave me a tour of the clinic. The clinic was 1 block from the main street and on an unpaved road. It was surrounded by a fence and a young hired guard opened the gate for the jeep to enter the clinic compound. The clinic and living quarters were attached, so the nurse did not have far to walk to attend the clinic. There was also staying on the compound, temporarily the principal of the school operated by the church in Makale. He stayed there with his wife and young daughter. Due to the emergency of the famine a small warehouse had been constructed behind the clinic in which were stored relief supplies: food, blankets, and clothing. A small shed that was to be a kitchen had been constructed as well which was used to prepare a cooked food ration for use in a twice daily feeding program, and a place to wash the bowls used to feed our patients. Two blocks away, there was also a small church building that was part of our church's mission in Makale. In the surrounding area on the edge of the city, there were additional NGOs operating. The International Red Cross, Catholic Relief Services, and Africare were the organizations we were to have the most contact with in the future. Our relief agency was called ADRA-Adventist Development and Relief Agency. They would send supplies and also a jeep to help our mission's work in Makale.

I was immensely impressed at the compassion and ingenuity of the nurse running the clinic. She was treating the illness she could treat in the clinic, as well as giving away clothing, and blankets. During the twice a day feeding, cooked food was given to the 100 or so registered to be fed, even though the space was limited. Those hired to work in the kitchen used a grain, powdered milk and edible oil, mixed together and used to make a porridge which looked like oatmeal, as has been noted before. It was a nourishing mixture fed to the children and some adults using plastic bowls. It was like eating a bowl of oatmeal at home. It was impressive because it saved lives in a simple, but efficacious manor.

Those who attended the clinic at that time included permanent residents of Makale (who were more "affluent" in a poor country), and those displaced by the famine who were going everywhere they could to get help. The residents of Makale resented those from the countryside as they feared the contagion they brought with them. This was a legitimate concern, but we did all we could to help everyone.

The two days I spent at Makale were inspiring and motivated me to do more to help. The nurse there was to leave soon. We had no replacement at a time when the clinic operation was critical with so many people coming for help. Later the decision was made by me and the Ethiopian Union Mission committee that we were going to send in rotation, nurses from other parts of the country to staff the clinic until a permanent nurse could be found. At the time this decision was made, I had no idea the impact this was to have on me and my family.

I returned to Addis Ababa to be with my wife and children. I also returned with some misgivings to my office on the Ethiopian Union Mission headquarters compound. I was also able to work to try to get funds, and projects going in the eight clinics and one hospital I was responsible for. I wrote proposals to get funds and one gratifying project was one to get vaccines to immunize children against measles, mumps, rubella, polio, and tetanus. We were going to try to get this outreach going in all of our health facilities. I worked hard also to send needed medical supplies to all of our health care workers.

I still had insomnia. I was thinking about the people I saw in Makale and it was hard to sleep when dwelling on what was happening there.

During the first two weeks in October 1984, two temporary nurses were sent to work in the relief operation in Makale. They were relieved by a male nurse subsequently. During November a female nurse was sent and I had planned to go to relieve her. It was my turn to operate the clinic. I informed my wife that I needed to go and I told her I would be gone for about one month. I was going to man the clinic in Makale and have the current nurse return to her own clinic in the southern part of the country. I warned my wife of this. There was still no permanent replacement for the nurse who had departed, so I was uncertain how long I would live and work in Makale. I did not know it at the time when I had made the trip back to Makale, but it would be 3 months before I saw my wife Alfredia, and my children Kellie and Kevin again.

The Face of Hunger

With great reluctance, I made the trip from our missionary home in Addis Ababa to Bole International Airport. With my travel documents in order and after giving my family a last kiss and embrace, I boarded the C-130 military plan to fly back to Makale. Once again, I fought off severe nausea during the flight, and I was still able to appreciate how beautiful the countryside looked from the air. There were the cultivated patchworks of farmland. I wondered what it would be like to live in one of those isolated villages which were at times perched on high plateaus. We could see no signs of drought or of the armed conflict going on in Tigray province. I was going to be about 473 miles from Addis Ababa. If anything happened to my family, I could only travel by aircraft to be with them as I had already learned before.

I was picked up by the driver and I checked in at the clinic before going back to the nearby hotel to stay until the nurse on duty left for her own clinic in the south.

Now the clinic was mine. I was responsible also for the warehouse, the jeep, the kitchen, and the feeding program. The people that resided permanently in Makale came for care. However, those displaced by the famine also came for care. The two groups of people would not come to the clinic and sit in the same waiting room I quickly discovered. I developed a schedule. In the afternoon, I would see only the displaced people, and in the morning, the local Makale residents. The people in the morning could pay for their care although this mostly involved paying for medicine we dispensed. The famine victims were of course utterly penniless, and I saw about 70 of them each afternoon the clinic was operating.

I am trained in the field of internal medicine, which meant for the most part the non-surgical care of adult patients. I quickly learned that about two-thirds of my patients were infants and children. They are the most vulnerable anyway during a time of calamity and famine. I had no x-ray, and no laboratory. I had to do the best I could to make a diagnosis on my patients by talking to them or their parents and by inspecting them and using simple instruments like stethoscopes, flashlights, otoscopes, thermometers and my hands. I for the most part could not refer patients to the local hospital as that hospital was deluged already. I could not speak the local language Tigrinya or the official national language Amharic so I was dependent on my translator. This of course made it challenging to get an accurate history on patients, but somehow, we managed.

Not long after I was on duty in the clinic, we received a visit from a local political leader. He was the head of the *kebele*, which I suppose would be akin to a home owner's association although far more repressive to residents. He told me his concerns with large numbers of the displaced people coming into our/his neighborhood which meant they might be bringing contagion to the area. He said: "These are our brothers and sisters, but we are concerned about them coming into our area, passing their waste, and maybe bringing sickness into the place we have to live in." He was very articulate and spoke good English. I had to admit that he was making a valid point. Our clinic had been present in Makale long before the present famine and there was no plan originally that the clinic would be a famine relief center. The clinic was not far from the center of town, while all the other relief organizations were operating at the periphery of the city. Outside the city was the large camp for the displaced people which contained maybe 36,000 people with thousands more needing relief as well. There were feeding centers, and relief tent hospitals on the periphery of the city. I tried to explain to the *kebele* leader that essentially, we had no choice but to take care of those people coming to us, and we could in no way turn them away. Our plan was to keep things as clean as we could around the clinic. He seemed to understand our intent and reluctantly agreed. I suppose he had the power to close down our clinic, but thankfully he did not do this.

The Face of Hunger

I was very disturbed that due to circumstances beyond my control, I seemed imprisoned as it were in Makale. It was good that I had not foreseen on arrival that I would not be able to see my family for 3 months. If I had known this, I might have taken drastic measures to end the separation. I could have just closed the clinic, got on a relief plane to Addis Ababa, and just told the officials in charge in Ethiopia, and back in America that I and my family resigned and we were going back home. I would then just demand we be sent back home. I had not had a warm relationship with the brethren in the Ethiopian Union Mission office, as I noted before. I felt like the attempts to find permanent missionaries for the Makale Adventist Clinic were too feeble. I felt like my being there was punitive. I began to think however about where I was, and about the immense suffering going on around me and in other places in Ethiopia. I realized by God's grace that I could actually help people, save lives and in some measure make a difference in the place I was serving. I then felt ashamed at my self-pity and my anger, even if this seemed justified. I decided that I was going to just focus my attention on the task at hand and do what I knew I had to do. After all that is why I came.

    I did have tools to help me. I had medicine to dispense. I had a small warehouse behind the clinic with food, blankets, and clothing to give away. I had also obtained some other items such as bars of soap, and bags of IV fluid to give IV infusions as I thought best. I had as it were weapons in an arsenal to fight the fight against disease and starvation. I also had allies in relief workers in the other relief organizations working in Makale. These people gave me medicine and other supplies to help in my mission work there. To this day I am thankful beyond words for their assistance.

    I buried myself in my work, but I tried to call as needed to check on my family. There was no e-mailing or text messaging in 1984 in Makale, so I kept in contact with my wife and children by telephone as needed. This did help me to get through a difficult and bittersweet experience.

My wife was going to be busy caring for our young children, and I was not going to be there to help. In addition, she was to help run some important functions of my office in Addis Ababa such as procuring and sending supplies as needed to the hospital and the clinics. Just another task we never thought would ever be necessary.

The events of a typical day working in the clinic, and our relief operation is forever fixed in my memory with vivid and surprising details. The intervening years have not seemed to change these memories substantially.

Each morning, before daybreak, I was awakened by the alluring singsong chanting delivered by a loudspeaker from a nearby minaret. It was a call to prayer for the true believers of Islam. I slept a bit longer, but soon I had to arise to get ready for a day of work in the clinic. I tarried there in my living quarters which consisted of one large room and a separate bathroom. I had no refrigerator, stove, or even eating utensils. I did have a hot plate and a large pan to boil some water. I then used a large basin in which I mixed the heated water and cold tap water to bathe. I had my own morning prayer session, then ate breakfast which oddly enough consisted of high energy biscuits which was the same thing we were feeding the famine victims. I was essentially having bread and water for breakfast.

I walked the short distance to the clinic and was greeted in the waiting room by the staff and a few patients. Prior to anything else being done, I read from the Bible and had a brief devotional thought translated into the local language by a local church leader, then prayer for the clinic.

For the next 4 hours or so I saw patients in the clinic who were local permanent residents of Makale. They were for the most part able to pay for the medication we dispensed. They usually had relatively minor illnesses such as diarrhea, colds, minor skin infections, joint pain, and complaints of tape worm (related to the habit of eating raw beef in Ethiopia). Occasionally patients had more serious illnesses such as an elderly woman we treated successfully for pneumonia with penicillin injections.

The most striking observations I made of all of our patients who came was the paucity of really elderly people. In addition, few were obese. I saw virtually no one with high blood pressure, or diabetes that I was able to detect. Perhaps two-thirds of my patients were young children. I was used to a much older age group back home with chronic health condition such as diabetes, high blood pressure, heart disease, arthritis, and obesity. The HIV/AIDS pandemic had not yet afflicted Ethiopia. It was not even discussed by the international medical community in Ethiopia.

In the morning, the first of two sessions of the feeding program were conducted. This had been set up months before I arrived and it functioned well. In fact, I was quite impressed with the plan. About 100 people had been registered. We could not handle much more than that. Names and ages had been recorded in a book that was given to me. At the appointed time in the morning, the gates to the clinic were opened and those we could help were admitted into our large compound. I was able to go out even in the midst of seeing patients in the clinic and observe things. The people filed into the yard in an unhurried and orderly manner. They would sit down and wait patiently to be fed. I noted the thin wasted bodies of the children, and some of the adults. They were dressed in what looked like burlap material. Some of the children were almost naked and covered by thin and frayed sheets of cloth. Most of the people were mothers and children. Some of the children were breast fed, but I wondered how much milk their obviously malnourished mothers could produce.

There was a small "kitchen" there where the food was prepared. The food was porridge like mixture which was a combination of grain-like oatmeal, edible oil, and powdered milk. It was served in a generous-sized plastic bowl, and a spoon was also provided. In addition, along with the bowl of food, we also gave a packet of the "high energy biscuits". They looked like large brown crackers, and there were about 5 of these in a packet. I never tasted the porridge, but I ate many of the biscuits, as I had to. They had a pleasant somewhat sweet taste.

After feeding the people, the staff cleaned the bowls and spoons. They were diligent workers and received a small stipend and food for their work. They kept the grounds as immaculate as possible. None of the staff had medical training and some only had an elementary school education. I will always be grateful for the great compassion they showed to those in the feeding program.

When I went out to look at the crowd we were feeding I would look around carefully to see if I could find any who were really acutely ill or seemed in dire need. I was shocked once to see a mother breast feeding a child who had a large open area on the scalp about 2-3 inches in size. The child's bony skull was visible in the shallow open area. The child was dreadfully thin, but his mother tried her best to breastfeed her baby. Our strategy was to feed the mother so she could feed her child. Unfortunately, the baby did not survive very long after I first saw him. On another occasion, I saw a small girl in her mother's arms who was actually having "agonal" respirations there on the compound. This is a pattern of breathing one has just before dying. We quickly grabbed the little girl and took her into the clinic. I started an IV and gave her more than 100 cc of 5 percent dextrose in normal saline. Amazingly, the little girl seemed to revive quickly, but she was a severely malnourished little girl. I wished I could have placed her in a hospital where she could get intensive care. We tried to help the mother give her feeding through breast milk and whatever else she would take, but little Abrehet, as she was called, died two days later. There were just too many like her that had even the relief hospitals filled to capacity at that time. I was still very upset about losing her.

I was dismayed and horror struck that from time to time children would actually die in our feeding program while on the compound. They would just die suddenly while in their mother's arms. The signal for this was the abrupt wailing of a mother who had just lost her child. We had a group of four men who were in our feeding program and who were designated by the nurse I relieved as the "funeral men". They received food for the onerous task of taking away the bodies of the young children with their mother's consent for burial.

It was however, gratifying to see how many of the children in our feeding program thrived and gained weight. I realized that the food we were feeding them in all likelihood contained more calories than they were used to eating even before the present food crisis had prevailed. This success was a reason for some sense of triumph in the midst of dreadful circumstances. In addition to the food, we made sure every child had a warm covering and we gave mothers blankets, and if they would fit, some of our donated clothing. The nights could be cool in Makale, a rainstorm any time of day could be chilling, and in fact life-threatening due to possible hypothermia

After the morning session of the clinic and the feeding session, I would take the short walk up the hill to the hotel where I had to eat. A number of relief workers, journalists, and other expatriate visitors stayed there. The accommodations were anything but luxurious, but there was nowhere else I could eat. I did envy groups such as the Catholic Relief Services who had a large compound with impressive trailers where their workers could sleep and eat from their own food supply.

At the hotel I would eat with the other relief workers who were from the US, Europe, and one I met from New Zealand. We would swap stories, and experiences. We gave each other encouraging words. I looked forward every day to this camaraderie. The evening meal was more of the same. The food was Western style and palatable. Unfortunately for me the food I had eaten there would later prove to be my undoing.

In the afternoon we had the second session of our feeding program. In the clinic itself, I was to see the people I had really come to Ethiopia to see—those displaced by the famine. At the appointed time in the afternoon, the people assembled outside our clinic compound. They looked different from the local residents of Makale. The local Makale resident's attire was more like those of us who live in the west, but these visitors now to our clinic were dressed in the garb of peasants from the countryside. The women had their hair braided in a similar fashion. Their clothes were of the same burlap cloth but looked like they had not been washed for weeks if ever. They wrapped themselves at times in a shawl like covering called a Gabi. The little ones were wrapped in a thin sheet of cloth, and often the young toddlers were almost nude. They were attended by a large cloud of buzzing flies. What I was seeing were the same people I had seen on television months before back in California. These were the poorest of the poor. They had been turned into nomads due to the drought and poverty. In my view, they were still patients to be treated with the same dignity as the more affluent patients who were permanent residents of Makale and those I took care of back in America.

During that afternoon session in the clinic, I saw usually about 70 patients, and most of these were infants and young children five and under. I saw these patients in a different room of the clinic than the larger room used for the patients seen in the morning. I had a chair to sit in during the examination, and there was a chair for my translator and bench for the mothers and children to sit on. One by one they came into the small examining room. I looked at each one of those children individually and examined them most of the time while they were still in the arms of their mother. The children were all cachectic and were often too weak to cry. I touched all those children, no matter how unclean they were. I could see the flies crawling on their faces, and bodies. I could see lice at times crawling on the tattered clothing or the wraps they wore. Those lice carried deadly diseases such as typhus and relapsing fever. I touched the children without gloves. I was not reckless in my view; I just wanted to be able to do a better exam. In retrospect, I might have done things differently, but I thought I was doing what I needed to do. At times I even held the children in my arms. I tried to get as close a look at them as I could.

The Face of Hunger

When I tried to take a brief history on the children, the mothers frequently just requested food. I was not able to take any more people into our feeding program as we were filled to capacity. I could not give more food, and that was sad. I realized that the mothers would just take their children to another relief agency for help. I did liberally give children a 200,000 IU dose of vitamin A to as many kids as possible, by piercing the capsules and dripping it into the child's mouth. I had learned that vitamin A besides helping with vitamin A eye disease played a role in a suppressed immune system thus making the children more prone for diarrhea and pneumonia. However, nourishing food is what they really needed, but I could not supply this in sufficient quantities. I felt overwhelmed by this, but I realized all I could do is to help as many of those children and their mothers as I could.

I did have a lot of blankets, and I learned that blankets saved lives. The malnourished kids often died of hypothermia (low body temperature). I gave away a lot of blankets. The clothes we had, which we gave away liberally, were less useful for the kids as they were much too large. I was awestruck that a simple small blanket could be lifesaving. Another thing that was of great benefit was bars of soap. When I examined some of the toddlers and older children, I noticed how utterly unclean their hands were. In fact, they would develop multiple pustules between their fingers, and on the palms of the hands. I gave their mothers bars of soap and told them to find a way to just wash the kid's hands until the pustules went away. I had no idea how they would be able to do this as clean water was in short supply in our area. It was not feasible to give them the antibiotic medication we had on hand. To my utter amazement, those mothers found a way to wash their kid's hands. I did not ask how or where the water came from. I saw some of those children back and to my relief, the pustules would be gone! I know it might have been just a temporary reprieve, but at least for the moment, there was some therapeutic success.

I gave away as many of the high energy biscuit packets as I could, but I had to do this carefully as I would have been besieged. I was grateful for all of the supplies sent to us such as bags of grain, and powdered milk. USA for Africa sent us the very best medication, mostly antibiotics which were a critical need.

I did not have to spend much time during the afternoon operation of our feeding program as I had already taken a look at things earlier in the day. Amazingly, after seeing all of the displaced people in the afternoon, our clinic waiting room was filled with scores of buzzing flies. I would take a can of insect spray and make a mist in the air to kill all the flies, sweep them up into a small pile and discard it. I thought about how dreadful it must have been for the people to live with that vermin along with the lice, the nighttime cold, lack of food, proper shelter, toilets, clean water, and just a measure of human comfort. I realized that at times my touching all of those unwashed patients was at times just a symbolic act as I could not supply all their needs. I just tried to help as many as I could.

We had cholera in Ethiopia when I was there in Makale. Cholera is a disease caused by a bacterium that finds its way into contaminated food and water. It appears during times of calamitous disasters such as earthquakes, floods, and typhoons. It lurks where there is overcrowding, congestion and a lack of proper sanitation. Those displaced by the famine and living as they were out of desperation in the camps in Ethiopia were a most vulnerable population. It was hard to get a lot of accurate information about cholera in Ethiopia at that time. This is because the government officials did not want us foreigners to use the word cholera, as it might make it more difficult to sell their coffee—the major cash crop. We were informed that the term cholera was forbidden. Instead we were to use the term: "severe diarrheal disease." This seemed inappropriate to us relief workers as cholera is in fact severe diarrheal disease and if it had in fact been recognized-appropriate intervention was needed.

My attitude was as the expression is now:" whatever"! I was determined to do what I had to do without a lot of talk. There is a vaccine for cholera and antibiotics can be used as well. I was not set up to give these things to a large number of but I was able to give IV fluids as needed. I had no other trained medical people to help me there in the clinic. Fortunately, I did not see very many people who were acutely ill.

Those of us in the clinic had a dramatic and tragic depiction of the plague that was in Makale. One day as happened from time to time we heard loud wailing coming from the street in front of our clinic. We ran out to see what was happening and saw a family there in the throes of grief. A little girl had died, who had been about 10 years of age. The family for some reason had walked a long way to get to our clinic, even though there were other medical/relief facilities that might have been closer to them. We were told that the young girl had gotten up that morning and seemed well. She then developed profuse diarrhea and vomiting which was intractable. The family decided to rush the little girl to get help as she had gotten very weak. It was only about four hours since the child had taken ill. However, just prior to arriving at our clinic, this young patient had taken her last breath. There was nothing we could do. The tragedy of this youngster's death is that it was preventable. If only they had sought medical attention earlier that child might be alive today. This just served to illustrate that fact that all too often preventable death and suffering abounded in our city and elsewhere in Ethiopia. Cholera is not an untreatable disease.

There were some we were able to save by IV infusions. It was not a large number, but enough to realize that our clinic was making a difference. One day one of the "funeral men" brought his wife to us. She was very weak from vomiting and diarrhea. We had a big shock in that as she sat down on the bench in the separate exam room used in the afternoon, she suddenly became almost unconscious and had a brief seizure. She was very dehydrated and near death. We laid her down on the floor and I immediately started an IV and gave her two liters of Dextrose in normal saline. Fortunately, she revived and later made a complete recovery. If I had not had the ability to give the IV fluids, we would have seen another preventable death.

It seemed like plague and contagion was all around me. There was the possibility of my contracting typhus, relapsing fever, cholera, TB and who knows what else. I tried to keep my clothes, my body, my living quarters, and the clinic as clean as possible. However, I thank God that I survived and stayed healthy with all the transmissible disease around me. However, I was not going to be totally unscathed as I found out later.

Relief workers stick together. This included expatriates, as well as Ethiopians involved with the relief efforts. I suppose it was like the relationship among soldiers who formed an attachment when under fire. The bond we had transcended culture, ethnicity, and language. It was a fraternity working together in the midst of the immense human tragedy we were witnessing. We shared together the latest news going around in the country. We heard reports as noted such as the one that the central government was hostile to our use of the word cholera even in the face of the many cases of profuse diarrhea poor sanitation and lack of clean drinking water that existed. We treated those patients as aggressively as we could. We heard that the "therapeutic" feeding centers around Makale which gave the most severely malnourished children just liquid feeding got very poor results and such efforts were discontinued. It seems that what we were doing in our feeding program in my clinic was desirable. At any rate, we learned the sad fact that when a child reached a certain state of malnutrition there seemed to be a point of no return and no matter what type of feeding you gave, it was to no avail. We gave what the kids would take, and strongly encouraged breast feeding by mothers. We gave out what we call "rehydration packets" for mothers to try to orally replenish by mouth fluids lost by children with diarrhea and vomiting. This was a great challenge given the lack of resources available in terms of containers to make up the solution using the packets and inadequate clean water.

I met many compassionate and caring people working in the midst of the crisis. That included the workers in my clinic, some of the government officials, and people in various organizations such as: Africare, Catholic Relief Services, the International Red Cross, World Vision and others. We were able to socialize at times as when we met together for meals in the nearby hotel. Once we had a social meeting hosted at the compound of the Catholic Relief Services. I was picked up by one of the nurses and while we were on our way, we stopped on a hill overlooking the camp set up to house the many thousands of people displaced by the famine. I remarked about how wonderful it was that we relief workers were there to help. She said: "No, Conner. What we are doing here in the face of all the misery here is nothing!" We continued on to our social gathering. We were offered some food, and alcoholic beverages-the latter I declined. At one moment during the gathering we suddenly and spontaneously started singing the old civil rights song; "We Shall Overcome." It was a very touching moment. I felt it was a privilege just to be there with them working to do what we could do to help. I personally did not feel a sense of futility. I knew for a fact that my clinic by God's grace had saved lives. I also thought about how many more would have suffered and died if all of us relief workers had not been there.

I spent Christmas 1984 in Makale. I was upset about being there and away from my wife and children. However, it was not safe for them to be there with me, and besides my children were in school in Addis Ababa. The clinic was closed on that day, but I spent time reading and cleaning, and rearranging some things in the clinic.

I did not know it at the time, but I would spend a total of 6 months in Makale. I was able to go home after 3 months; I was relieved by an Ethiopian nurse we were able to contact. I had to return for 3 more months for a total of six months spent in Makale and away from my family until our permanent missionary family, was in place. I thanked God they arrived to their duty station.

I can look back now and just note that this bittersweet experience changed me for the better. My wife and I will always consider ourselves as missionaries. We were never the same after our experiences.

Mothers and Children in our Feeding center in Makale

The Warehouse on the Makale Clinic Compound

The "Kitchen" on the Makale Clinic compound

Food Grain for Those in Need

A Challenging trip

Traveling to a Remote Village

A view of the Relief Camp in Makale

An aerial view of the Ethiopian Countryside

Healthy Ethiopian children

Community Outreach in the Denver Metro Area

"The Inner City Health Center" - A Place To Help The Uninsured

Family Portrait before the Trip to Ethiopia

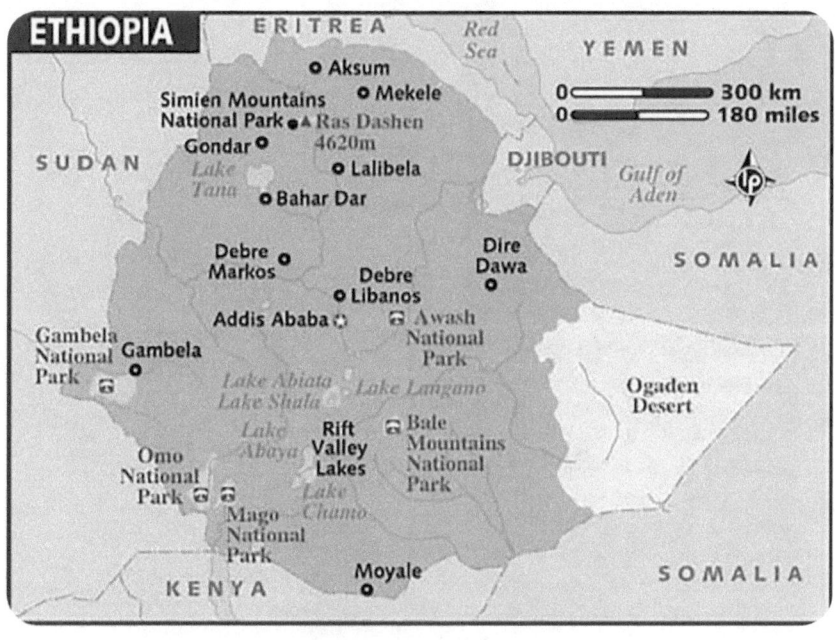

A Letter To My Mother

The Seventh-day Adventist Church
ETHIOPIAN UNION   P. O. Box 145   ADDIS ABABA
Cable "Adventist"

November 18, 1985

Dear Mother,

    I hope that this letter finds everyone doing well. We are all well. As I write this letter Fredia is busy writing a newsletter that we are going to make copies of to send to almost everyone we know. Kevin and Kellie are reading as usual. (Both of them are real book worms and are doing well in school.) We are listening to the song "We are The World". Here in Ethiopia we really appreciate this song and all the money that was raised. We received a large amount of donated medicine that was labeled "USA for Africa" and it was a real blessing because we have many very sick people to contend with.

    I am back in Addis now. I think I told you earlier that I have been away from Fredia and the kids for a total of five months this year. We had a serious staffing problem and there was no replacement to work in our clinic in Makale. Makale is a city located about 800 kilometers northeast of Addis. During my time in Makale I operated the clinic (which took care of anywhere from 30-70 patients per day) and supervised our small feeding center which cared for about 400 people. I don't know if you are aware of it but probably some of the films you saw on T.V. were from Makale. There were several large relief camps on the outskirts of the city which gave shelter to about 50,000 people displaced by the drought. These camps were full of misery and suffering. Quite often there were film crews from Britain, the U.S., and Canada coming to take pictures.

The Seventh-day Adventist Church
ETHIOPIAN UNION P. O. Box 145 ADDIS ABABA

Telephone 15 85 90
Cable 'Adventist'

Working in our clinic in Makale was a real experience. Most of my patients were drought affected people with serious malnutrition. Most of the children I saw were skeletons and were in desperate condition. Many of them were dying from diarrhea and dehydration. We saw a number of very serious diseases such as cholera, typhus, typhoid fever and tuberculosis. Almost all of our poor patients had serious skin infections just from not being able to wash. Their clothing was often just rags. So you can see that we were dealing with people who were among the most destitute in the world and who were the poorest of the poor. Many times people were brought into the clinic in shock and near death. I had to give people IV's right in the clinic. Many times I used our jeep to take people to the hospital. I can tell you that it was really heart breaking and almost overwhelming to see so many people who were homeless, hungry and practically naked. The needs of the people seemed to far exceed the resources of all the various relief agencies working in Makale. Finally things did improve. The people were given food supplies to take home with them so they left Makale and returned to their villages. Then the camps were closed for the most part. There are still many sick people for us to care for in Makale, but conditions are better. We should thank God for all of this.

I am very busy trying to plan all of the activities for my department for 1986. One of my major programs will be to try to begin an immunization program for children here because this is an urgent need.

The Seventh-day Adventist Church
ETHIOPIAN UNION   P.O. Box 145   ADDIS ABABA
Telephone 15 85 00'
Cable 'Adventist'

    Kellie and Kevin are doing well in school. They go to a school which is actually better than any school Kellie had in the U.S. They are learning French, and meeting children from all over the world. Fredia is *very* busy doing a number of things including helping me in my office. By this point in time we have adjusted quite well to living here. You know we have been here for 15 months now.

    We will try to write more often in the future. I would like to ask you if you could send us the adult sabbath school quarterly (by air mail) with one regular adult quarterly and one teacher's quartely. Also would you send me six tubes of "chop-stick"! Please wrap the chopstick well so it will not tear the bag. Let us know how much the postage is, and we will send you a check. Tell everyone we said hello.

                                Love,
                                  Byron

Expired Medicine?- No Thanks!

❈

"Every good act is charity. A man's true wealth hereafter is the good that he does in this world to his fellows."

Moliere

IMAGINE THAT HERE IN America you hear and see riveting reports about a disaster such as the famine in Ethiopia. You and your church or another community group decides that you feel compelled to send supplies and equipment to help. The question is what to send? Having been on the receiving end of such philanthropy, I would just like to give some advice about what to send and what not to send.

One of the most helpful things to do is to find out what a recipient might want if possible. This recipient might be a government health ministry, a church group, a clinic, a hospital or an aid organization. Perhaps just doing some investigation might lead to a donation that would be most encouraging and might be a real beneficent gift to a person working on the front lines in a human catastrophe. Failure to think and plan carefully might result in the sending of equipment or medication that is of limited or no benefit to a recipient.

Before I mention my greatest concern-which is medication, let me first talk about equipment. Just consider the fact that there is a significant difference in equipment used in a relief hospital (which might be a group of tents), a city/regional hospital and a clinic or dispensary. However, these facilities have one thing in common. If they receive donated equipment that was broken or useless in America, it will be useless in Africa. In that case despite the best of intentions, it is best not to send it. It was infuriating to receive some of the things that I have seen such as: equipment meant to be used with a voltage supply of 110 volts when 220 volts are what is available in the field; equipment needing spare parts to make them operable; and equipment more appropriate for a high-tech hospital in America.

I was on the receiving end of over 100 barium enema kits—all expired. First of all, the probability that a barium enema kit (used to do x-ray studies of the colon) would be used at all in most of Africa is remote. Second, no one in Ethiopia would use this expired equipment. We mostly needed equipment to help in famine relief, in my view. Hence such a shipment was an appalling waste of money and resources. I was very much disinclined to say thank you for such a shipment.

We had the sad experience of receiving a shipment sent with some fanfare by a church in America. The shipment was worth about $100,000. When we received it, the first thing I looked at was the packing list. I was dismayed to find that most of this shipment was useless. We received things such as a large number of expired capsules used to treat the common cold. In addition, there was a sizable amount of large blue vitamin tablets about one-half the size of an adult's thumb. It would have been hard to imagine a weak, starving child swallowing such a tablet, and benefitting from it. We did receive some acetaminophen tablets we were able to use. However, I had to restrain myself from writing back to the church that sent this shipment and tell them even in a diplomatic way that what we received was mostly useless. If only the people who donated equipment and medication to us had just asked us what we needed it would have avoided an unfortunate situation.

Once I sent a requested list of medications which we needed to use in our famine relief, but to my dismay, this list was ignored and I still received a largely poorly conceived shipment. It seemed like an exercise in futility. I even had a visit from the individual largely responsible for what was shipped to us. He was outraged when I told him that we received inappropriate shipments. I was outraged that he was outraged! Needless to say, that was not a productive meeting.

Prior to traveling to the mission field, I had spoken once with a former and returning missionary physician. He told me that when he was serving once in Africa he had used expired antibiotics such as penicillin. He mentioned that he had used the expired medication and had just doubled the dose of penicillin if used to treat his patients. That seemed like an irrational approach to patient care in my view. I also questioned the ethics of doing such a thing. How could you be sure that the medication would do what you think it should do? I did not try to remonstrate with this missionary, but I could have asked if he would treat his patients in America with expired antibiotics? Are the lives of people in Africa worth so little that using such expired medication was acceptable? I discovered that having a potential paucity of supplies was no excuse. I was blessed in that I was always able to obtain, often from multiple sources the medication I needed to give good care to my patients. I made absolutely certain, that none of this medication was expired or inappropriate for the patients I was treating. I had to be sure of the best therapeutic outcome. My conscience would not allow me to do otherwise. I simply refused to believe that medications that are expired are worthwhile even if some supposedly authoritative entity claims that they are. As it turned out, I had some experiences that made me thankful I was adamant in using the best medication possible-even in a poor third world country. Look at three case histories as described below.

Case history: A patient with pneumonia:

The translator who worked with me in my clinic in Makale was a young woman in her 30's with three children. Her husband was in Germany at the time. She was also 7 months pregnant when she fell ill. She had worked in the clinic for years as a translator and was a caring, compassionate worker. I highly valued her assistance in our clinic as we cared for victims who had been displaced by the famine as well as patients who were residents of Makale. I will call my translator Ayana to protect her identity.

Ayana came to the clinic one day and just mentioned that she was not feeling well. Since she was not a complainer I thought that she needed attention. I was not sure what was wrong at first for certain, but one sign I noted is that she had a cough. I listened to her lungs and noted some scattered abnormal sounds which were however subtle. What she needed was an x-ray to rule out pneumonia. The only place to get an x-ray in Makale was the local hospital. I hoped that whatever was found did not mean a hospital admission as it was not my opinion that inpatients at that hospital got good care, perhaps just due to lack of equipment. Another concern that had been expressed to me by local people was that the hospital gave priority to military patients at the expense of civilians. I had no firm proof this was true, but I still had misgivings about anyone I knew being admitted to that hospital.

My driver and I took Ayana to the hospital emergency room. The x-ray was taken and to my dismay revealed a serious finding. She had a patchy pneumonia (bronchopneumonia) that involved a significant portion of her right lung. In my view, Ayana had a potentially life-threatening illness. Despite this, she did not want to be treated in the hospital, and I agreed with this. I was going to have to treat her in the clinic.

I was thankful beyond words that I had some injectable penicillin in the clinic which I was able to use to treat Ayana. It was something I did not think I would be using. This penicillin was not expired and I felt comfortable that it would be potent. I told Ayana that we would treat her twice daily with intramuscular penicillin injections which I would give myself, as there was no one else to do this who worked in our clinic. I did not have a nurse.

Ayana spent the first day of her treatment in our clinic, attended by me and the guard for our clinic. My living quarters were attached to the clinic. I could hear her moaning in discomfort due to her illness most of the night. I came by to check on here during the night. One of Ayana's family members stayed by at home with her children.

Ayana felt like going home the second day of her treatment and did so. She improved during the next week, and actually reported to return to work before the ten days of treatment was finished. She was grateful and I was thanking God as the outcome could have been different. She later told a nurse who worked in our clinic after my stay there that I had saved her life. I look back in retrospect and shudder with the thought that perhaps she might have lost her life if I had not treated her with the appropriate medication. I was pleased that I was adamant about using expired medication and had full confidence that what I used would be potent enough to have a more predictable, and desirable outcome. All of us treating people in difficult situations should have the same confidence in what we are doing. This just reinforced my convictions about the necessity if just doing the right thing in treating a patient astutely and ethically no matter where they are and who they are.

Case History: A patient with an arm infection:

A young lady presented herself to our clinic in pain and obvious distress. She showed us her right arm and it was grossly red and swollen above and below the elbow joint. She had had some type of injury to her elbow. I was concerned that she had an infection inside the elbow joint itself. I decided that I needed to treat this arm infection like it was "cellulitis". This is a diffuse infection of the soft tissues. It can become potentially life threatening as the person with cellulitis can become "septic" (due to bacteria getting into the bloodstream). If we had been in America, I would have placed this patient in the hospital. She would have had a film of her arm and possibly an MRI film of the arm. I would have obtained a consultation from an orthopedic surgeon as well. As it was, hospital admission was just not going to happen, and the only physician who was going to see her was just me. I was going to have to treat her in the clinic as an outpatient.

Treatment options were limited. I had injectable penicillin, but I decided not to use this. I had obtained a large bottle of 500 mg cephalexin tablets due to USA for Africa who were very good about sending essential drugs to Africa, and not expired. I had plenty of these tablets and I was confident the medication was potent. I gave her enough medication to take 1 tablet four times daily for 10 days.

Daily she returned to the clinic to be reexamined. To my utter delight and gratitude to God, this patient had a complete recovery, and after treatment, one could not tell this young lady had had a potentially life-threatening infection. She was indeed fortunate that she was a local resident of Makale, and not a peasant displaced by the famine. In that case the outcome might have been different. The outcome would have been certainly less benign in my opinion if I had not had a potent antibiotic to use. I had treated her unlike I would have had we been in America, but the good outcome was gratifying beyond words.

Case History: Children with Vitamin A Deficiency Eye Disease:

While living in Makale, I frequently took walks around the town when the clinic was not open, just to get some exercise. As I was walking along the street one day I saw a pitiful figure sitting on the median strip of the road. It was a young girl about ten to twelve years of age. She had her hand outstretched and at the same time called out to people passing by asking for alms to help her. She was obviously blind. I drew near and looked at her to see what her problem was. The cornea of her eyes looked opaque and distorted. I could tell from my brief inspection while just walking by that this unfortunate child was a malnourished victim of the famine.

What she had was vitamin A eye disease with keratomalacia. What happens with this disease is that the tissues of the cornea break down, ulcers of the cornea develop with secondary infection and irreversible eye damage. This leads to permanent visual loss. The tragedy is that this type of visual loss is preventable by early intervention, with the most important remedy being providing needed food. Short of being able to feed all concerned, I learned that simple vitamin A supplementation might save a child from blindness in addition to other beneficial effects such as bolstering of the immune system to prevent diarrhea and pneumonia.

I had obtained some potent vitamin A gel capsules from the Helen Keller Institute. These capsules contained 200,000 international units of vitamin A. This medication could be given to a young child by puncturing the capsules with a needle and squeezing the contents into the mouth of the child.

I had noted when looking at the eyes of the young children brought in from the countryside that there were early signs of eye disease. I noted some discolored spots on the cornea although visual loss had not yet occurred. After receiving the vitamin A capsules, I started to use them on those with suspicious findings of eye disease. What I observed was that after only a single dose of 200,000 international units of vitamin A, those discolored spots on the corneas of the children simply disappeared. These children were spared for the moment from blindness. Once again, I experience the exhilaration of a good treatment outcome. I was again rewarded I believed for being able to give appropriate treatment to those in need. The treatment was simple, effective, and inexpensive. Even today I feel gratified that for that moment, we were able to help those children and prevent likely lifetime disability. I just have to trust that those children were able to get the proper nutrition to maintain their health.

Because of these experiences noted above, I am convinced that even in a poor third world country, and with limited resources we need to give the best care we can to everyone. We will be gratified for having done this and will have the best outcome.

A Near Death Experience

--- ❋ ---

"When you were born, you cried and the world rejoiced. Live your life in a manner so that when you die the world cries and you rejoice."

Native American Proverb

MANY EXPATRIATES CAME TO Ethiopia at the time my family and I resided there. As a rule, they came for altruistic and humanitarian purposes. These people came mostly from America, Canada, Asia, Europe, South America, the Caribbean and other countries in Africa. When you include the foreign embassies, people came from all over the globe. They came with good intentions and a desire to serve and help Ethiopia. They came to save lives and like me, may have been drawn by the poignant needs portrayed in the media. There was some risk involved and also there was the reality of uncertainty as to what they would find. There were some who gave their lives. There were many who suffered illness and I was one of those. I will recount my experience with illness, but first we need to consider the context.

It seemed to me that at times expatriates were almost reckless when they traveled to Ethiopia. We thought too little of the need to guard our health. We had at times an attitude of invincibility that we thought was magically conferred on us as we were humanitarians. The reality was that those who were wise took precautions to stay healthy. We were in fact exposed to a host of hazards that could be a threat to life and limb. If we were too reckless, and not diligent enough, we could experience a catastrophic illness, permanent disability or even death. The routine precautions that one should take are reasonable any time one is traveling abroad, whether it is too an industrialized or a developing country. I would just like to share some insights that I hope will help the reader have a safer and more productive stay abroad.

<u>Familiarize yourself with the country you are traveling to</u>: Learn as much as you can about the host country by doing some appropriate reading or talking if possible, with a native or someone who has visited the host country. Know the political system, demographics, weather, customs, history, and health issues extant. If you can learn as much of the language as possible since that will be an invaluable advantage.

<u>Pay attention to any pre-existing medical conditions you might have</u>: Chronic health conditions such as high blood pressure, diabetes, heart disease, serious obesity, arthritis, asthma, and others need planning and consideration. Don't assume medication you need will be readily available abroad. Don't ignore your family history, even if you are well. Family medical problems such as diabetes, heart disease, and cancer may require some type of screening especially if you will be abroad for years. See a doctor and dentist before your trip. Travel health insurance would be advisable if available.

<u>Do all needed prophylactic regimens and immunizations</u>: Be diligent about learning what vaccines and shots you and your family need prior to travel. These vaccines are going to be of more benefit than risk. They may protect you from potentially life-threatening diseases such as tetanus, polio, pertussis, yellow fever, and hepatitis. It is unwise to forego needed immunizations. In some countries, an expatriate has to take certain medication to prevent contracting malaria. This is important as malaria can be a cause of death or a

protracted or severe illness. Whatever prophylactic regimens are needed, follow them as advised. Again see a medical provider for assistance here.

Be aware of the most significant threats to your health and well-being: These may include traffic accidents, boating accidents, infectious diseases (food and water borne, sexually transmitted diseases), and violent crime. In a developing country in particular there are a host of infectious diseases that may be endemic such as hepatitis, tuberculosis, malaria, parasitic infections, diseases spread by vectors (such ticks, mosquitoes, flies, and lice) and bacterial infections that may cause severe diarrhea, skin infections and pneumonia. Use appropriate travel precautions when traveling by vehicle (use seat belts if available). Be wary traveling by boat. Be cautious about the safety of food and water you consume. Obviously unprotected sex is ill advised due to the threat of sexually transmitted diseases and HIV infection. Don't consider yourself immune to getting sick or injured.

I became very ill while I was in Ethiopia. Prior to my serious illness, I had the requisite minor episodes of diarrhea that I suspect all expatriates experience. The source of my illness was no mystery. It was the food I was forced to consume when I resided in Makale doing famine relief in the 6 months of my time there in 1984-1985. I did not actually become ill until shortly after I returned to Addis Ababa and reunited with my wife and children.

Shortly after my return home, I first noted something was amiss when I was walking to the mission headquarters one day after a taxi ride from home. Suddenly I felt mildly nauseated and very fatigued during my short walk. This sensation came on suddenly, although I had felt fine early that morning. When I arrived at the office, I felt feverish and ached all over. I was shocked when I looked in a mirror at the office and noted that the whites of my eyes were faintly yellow tinged alerting me to the fact that I was jaundiced and likely had hepatitis. I was very dismayed and alarmed at this. I called my wife and she came to pick me up to take me to our residence. I informed my superiors there that I was ill and would most likely be out of the office for some time.

When I arrived home, I went straight to bed. That is when what seemed like torture began. I began to experience unbelievably intense body aches (myalgia), that were unrelenting but waxed and waned. I had alternating fever and chills. I had a headache that came and went. Waves of nausea assailed me, and this made even just drinking water a challenge, let alone eating food.

The next day I went to a local laboratory we had found. I had a battery of liver tests done and they did in fact confirm that my liver enzymes were markedly elevated. I knew then I was in trouble. I could only surmise that I was in trouble. I was never able to discover while I was in Ethiopia exactly which type of hepatitis I had. Years later back in America, I found out that most likely what I had was hepatitis E which is similar to hepatitis A.

I lay in my bed at home praying for recovery and healing, and others were doing the same. In the meantime, I was terrified. I felt like I was dying.

I had some morbid thoughts about death and dying. The type of food and waterborne hepatitis I had was supposedly relatively benign with a low mortality rate. However, I did not feel like I had a benign illness. I could just imagine what the virus of hepatitis was doing to my liver. I was afraid that I was going to have a massive liver failure and die right there in Ethiopia. If I could have been transported back to America, and placed in an intensive care unit, the outcome more than likely would have been no better. Perhaps a liver transplant would have saved me, but the virus was in my bloodstream.

I was able to keep down little for about 2 days, and I was afraid I was going to get dehydrated. Actually, I was able to keep down enough fluids to keep from getting critically ill. As I lay there in bed I was amazed that I felt just as bad lying down as sitting up or walking around. The constellation of symptoms I had were almost overwhelming. There was a brief period of time when I actually wanted to die as then the pain and misery I was going through would be no more. However, I thought that if I died, by wife would be a young widow and I would be denied the experience of seeing my children grow up. My family back home would be devastated.

There was no medicine that was going to save or help me. My immune system had to fight off the virus, and for a while I was thinking the virus was going to prevail. I prayed again and again for healing, although I knew that the possibility of death was real. I was thinking that this was my reward for leaving home, and traveling to the other side of the planet because I had been moved and compelled by images of starvation I had seen on television. I was going to join a host of people who had come to Africa and succumbed to an endemic virus.

For one week I wallowed in misery. I was thinking any day now, I will lapse into a coma and that would be the end. I was thankful that it was unlikely that my wife and children would get what I had. However, I was thinking I would not be with them much longer anyway. I alternated between faith that God would heal me and a belief that my death was imminent.

I did see an American doctor at the start of my illness as required by the Ethiopian Union Mission president. The doctor just told me what I already knew-that I had hepatitis. Not surprisingly, he had nothing but best wishes to offer.

A ray of hope appeared about one week into the worst of my symptoms. I began to feel noticeably better. I was able to eat and drink a bit more, and the nausea diminished. I still felt very fatigued and a bit achy. I did not feel like venturing too far from my bed just yet, however, I no longer believed my demise was near. Repeat liver tests did in fact show improvement.

During my time on the sickbed, I relived the time I had spent in Makale. I was thankful for my experience in that city overall, although after being there, I was brought to the brink of death. Moreover, I thought I was now really a survivor. I had endured the long separation from my wife and children, and the shock and dismay of seeing so much suffering, death and misery of the people who I had served there in Makale. I was thankful that as I improved, I could dispense with my morbid thoughts of leaving this earth before my time. I would have been dead at the age of 38.

In retrospect now, I can say that it was a privilege to be in Ethiopia. There were hardships to be sure, and my illness was the ultimate adversity. Nevertheless, I am still among the living and I thank God for that. My wife and I both emerged with a determination to serve everyone that has been unquenchable.

The State of The World's Children

"Children are the living messages we send to a time we will not see."

John W. Whitehead

I TRIED TO HAVE a positive outlook on the situation and the work environment in Ethiopia. Although I was in-country nearly three years, the most meaningful and rewarding time I spent there was the 6 months I spent in Makale. When not in that city, I spent 1 month working at our mission hospital in Western Ethiopia in Wollega province in the city of Gimbie at Gimbie Adventist Hospital. I did inpatient and outpatient care. It was a very challenging and intimidating place to work, as often surgery was needed for our patients and all I could do was assist as needed. I had had no meaningful surgical training. I worked periodically at our clinic in Addis Ababa. I spent many hours writing proposals to various donors to get funds, medications and equipment for our medical work. I also spent time visiting offices of the Ministry of Health to do what we could do to collaborate with them on things such as an immunization project for children. I attended meetings which involved the international medical community at the Christian Relief and Development Association (CRDA) to discuss health and relief needs for the country. CRDA did fund an immunization project to give vaccines to children in our facilities for tetanus, measles, pertussis, polio, diphtheria, and TB. I traveled to all eight of our clinics and two of them required a hazardous journey using a four-wheel drive vehicle. To visit a site of a planned future clinic at a village called Fessa, I had to travel a significant distance by horseback. It was worth it, as I was eventually able to countersign a memorandum of understanding to start at new clinic at the Fessa village. I also traveled to Djibouti with a delegation of people from our church, to look into starting a dental clinic. I sensed that the administrators I worked with were disappointed that I did not do some things that they expected me to do. Those things included doing stop smoking seminars and also working to build a "Better Living Center" (to do health seminars as I saw it for the urban crowd) as noted before, on the main mission compound in Addis Ababa. I just could not bring myself to do those things as they seemed inappropriate given the true causes of suffering in Ethiopia. You might say I was defiant (in a passive-aggressive way) and tried to do what I believed to be the right things to do despite anyone's displeasure or disappointment. As far as I was concerned, I was following my conscience no matter what the consequences were. I had some leverage in that in being a physician if I was sent home on a punitive basis; I was not going to be unemployed when I got back home!

Altogether, I estimate I spent a total of about 8-9 months separated from my wife and children. I was and am grateful for a supportive and resourceful wife. She was an irreplaceable companion.

At times I got discouraged and depressed. I sought solace in prayer and Bible study. I was buoyed up by friendships with other missionaries who were members of my church, as well as some who belonged to other churches. I had Ethiopian friends as well who gave me much encouragement, by just being cordial and friendly. The expatriate community was a very efficacious support group.

The most amazing thing I found however is that I found comfort and enormous encouragement from a series of books I came across. I discovered these books on one of my visits to nearby offices of the World Health Organization, and also those of UNICEF-the United Nations International Children's Emergency Fund. I obtained as many books and journals as I could obtain and read as much as I could. The books I prized the most was an annual report called; the *State of the World's Children*. I obtained the reports for 1984-1987. I read each one repeatedly. UNICEF was established in 1946. The publications I came to value so much were first published in 1980 under the leadership of the UNICEF Executive Director James P. Grant. These books were an analysis of some global trends affecting the health and welfare of children. There were economic, social statistics, demographic facts, and health statistics for most of the world's nations (if they reported). There were reports on effectual health projects of selected countries from around the world. These reports gave one thoughts about projects we could consider implementing. Most importantly there were consensus reports of effective health care interventions for a poor third world country. These reports were immensely inspiring. I felt like somebody out there cared and had a passion to help those least able to defend and help themselves—children. I had guidance and support, and things I could try to emulate and put into practice. There were simple, cost effective, preventative measures that were proven to work in the developing world. It was to me like going to a rally or pep talk. I was amazed that those books had such an impact on me, but grateful that I had come across them.

We may see now appeals from some humanitarian organization in print, or on TV, but we do not understand the magnitude of the plight of children in impoverished countries, and even in wealthier countries. In poor countries a much larger proportion of the population is young. The infant and under five mortality rate is a good deal higher than in America. Children often die of undernutrition and infectious diseases. Now HIV infection is a major cause of mortality and morbidity which was not the case when I lived and worked in Ethiopia. Many children die from preventable causes as noted below. Now today when I see the appeals on TV to adopt a child in a third world country or to give funds to feed children, I am wishing that the someone somewhere would just sit down and study how they can really help the children abroad. It seems to me that we here in America and in other richer countries need to have the intellectual prowess to really figure out how we can do the most good. We need to really do things that are going to make a longer term and more meaningful impact.

I avidly read the annual reports of UNICEF, the *State of the World's Children*, as they told me what really helps the most. I wondered and I still do why we do not pay more attention to publications like this. Even today I think about those publications. If I were to go back to Ethiopia, those books would be on my reading list.

I would just like to summarize below the things I learned in review of the books I became familiar with for the years 1984-1987. However, the years beyond 1984 were reiterations in my view of the 1984 addition.

The State of the World's Children 1984:

"A revolution for children": The report proclaimed a breakthrough in some simple interventions that had the potential to save the lives of 7 million children each year worldwide. The focus of these interventions would be on children in the developing world. Many countries including: Bolivia, Britain, Canada, Columbia, France, Haiti, India, Pakistan, the Philippines, Sri Lanka, Sweden, Tanzania, Thailand, and the United States acknowledged the value of the plans. The gains in child welfare would be achieved at a relatively low cost, would require simple technology, and would be efficacious with notable results in a relatively short time. The overview of interventions would be as follows:

1) <u>Oral rehydration therapy</u> for treating a leading cause of death in the developing world-diarrhea with associated dehydration.

2) <u>Growth monitoring</u> which involved simple charts kept by the child's mothers to monitor monthly growth and to allow for early detection of malnourishment.

3) <u>Expanded childhood immunization</u> which entailed administering vaccines to prevent the six main immunizable diseases which included measles, polio, tetanus, pertussis, diphtheria, and tuberculosis

4) <u>Promotion of breastfeeding</u> which involved educating mothers about the value of this simple intervention crucial for the well-being of children.

5) <u>Additional techniques</u> which comprised family spacing and food supplementation.

I repeatedly read about the interventions noted which were already being used and that included to a large degree those involved with medical care to the children of Ethiopia and other developing countries.

Working in the clinic in Makale and for a good portion of my stay, I was caring for a transient displaced population, which was destitute and homeless. Because of this, it was difficult to implement the strategy described by UNICEF. Despite this it was intuitively obvious to me that the interventions described were of immense value. I decided that when I could I was determined to do all I could to be a part of "the revolution for children".

I thought about the children in our feeding program who had done well with just the food, clothing and medication we were providing. It was gratifying to see the benefits. We had been able to save some sick children and even some with severe marasmus had survived. However, in my clinic, we lost some as well, and that was painful to realize. We were trying to do the best we could in dreadfully challenging circumstances. It was encouraging to know that there was and are strategies to help our patients even with limited resources and a challenging limitation of needed infrastructure in terms of transportation and adequate medical facilities.

I continued my study of the UNICEF information as there was further elaboration on schemes to help the leading causes of death for children as noted below.

Treating diarrhea and dehydration in children:

It might be surprising for those of us living in an industrialized country to hear that diarrhea is a leading cause of death in poor countries. In the US we have clinics, and emergency facilities to take care of kids with diarrhea. Indeed, it would be distinctly unusual for a child in America to die of diarrhea. However, deaths due to diarrhea were the rule rather than the exception in countries of limited means such as Ethiopia. In fact, 5 million children worldwide die of diarrhea each year. The question is what is the remedy for this? The solution described in the *State of the World's Children 1984* publication was called: oral rehydration therapy or "ORT". This involved the spoon feeding of a child a mixture of salt, glucose and water using a bowl or a cup.

There are a host of organisms: bacteria, viruses and parasites that caused the diarrhea we saw in Ethiopia. The final common pathway for death was loss of essential bodily fluids, dehydration, prostration and death. Despite the diversity of the agents that cause infection, the treatment prescribed will be the same:-giving by mouth the lifesaving solution by spoon feeding the at risk child. We did not have means to do stool lab tests, and as a rule this was not needed. The goal will be to give about one cup of fluid for each loose stool. The solution can be made by using "rehydration packets" that are envelopes that are opened and added to a container. These are manufactured with the desired concentration to make up the fluid, salt and glucose that the child needs. The challenge is being able to instruct parents as to how to give the fluid replacement needed. There had to be a source of drinkable water, a clean container to make up the mixture and a safe stable environment for parents to give the treatment needed. In addition, the child still needed food. Regrettably, the displaced people I saw did not have all they needed to take care of their children. They were living on the streets of Makale, or in the camps on the outskirts of the city. They did not have any containers for water and for making the drink needed. There were no spoons or cups. We had to do the best we could. At times, I gave IV fluid in the clinic to the worst-off children, but this was infrequent given my lack of facilities to do this. We still gave the mothers rehydration packets to take with them with instructions. We were not able to do it, but parents can be instructed to make a rehydration mixture at home: mixing in 1 liter of water, 8 teaspoons of sugar, 1 teaspoon of salt and giving this in portions of one cup for each loose stool.

In a more stable situation where the child lives in a village, and there is accessible clean water, and a clinic, it is possible to have more successful treatment for diarrhea and dehydration. We hoped this would be the case when and if the famine was alleviated.

From 1984 on, to now we can look at the value of ORT. We can state now that it is in fact part of a "revolution for children". This low-cost technique costing about 33 cents per child can reduce the death rate from diarrhea by 60%. It can help to break the vicious cycle of diarrhea, malnutrition and death. Diarrhea is linked to under nutrition, poor weight gain, and increased risk of death

Protecting the growth and development of children:

In many nations across the developing world, techniques and strategies were promoted and used which had the potential to save millions of young lives:

- Growth monitoring which involved monthly weigh-ins for children to insure they were keeping pace and not falling off in the pace of their growth. The scheme was for the mothers to keep in their possession small cards with the imprinted growth charts which would act as an early warning system that a child was falling behind in growth. In a health center setting, intervention and counseling could be done.

- Food supplementation which involved making sure that pregnant mothers received adequate food which included locally grown fruits, vegetables, grains, legumes, milk and yoghurt, to allow for the healthy growth and the survival of their children. The most urgent goal was to prevent "low birth weight" of infants, as that significantly increased their mortality. Low birth weight was considered to be 2500 grams and was deadly. By insuring that mothers had about 2500 calories daily and gained about 12 kilos in weight, the scourge of low birth weight could be ameliorated. Low birth weight was associated with decreased resistance to infection, and increased risk of malnourishment of children. A mother who was malnourished had a decreased ability to lactate, which could be devastating to a growing young infant.
- Family spacing involved not just simply distributing contraceptive pills but attempts to make sure that there was an adequate period of time between pregnancies. It was discovered that if the interval between deliveries of a mother's children was less than two years, there was decreased survival. By the technique of some sexual abstinence there could be some stretching of the time interval between babies. However,

It had been found that a simple way to prevent too short a space between births was just by doing prolonged breast feeding. This was because breast feeding raised a mother's prolactin level which inhibited ovulation and thus another pregnancy. Thus, it might be possible to have an interval of about 2 years with this simple technique.

Expanded program of immunization:

This was an effort against six killer diseases and was found to increase child survival and prevention of disability. The desired immunizations were against diphtheria, whooping cough (pertussis), tetanus, measles, polio and tuberculosis. (Vaccinations against other diseases were to be added later such as hepatitis b, and Haemophilus influenza type b.) The challenge was to maintain the "cold chain" to get the vaccines to children. This could be a challenge in the face of poor roads and in remote places, but the benefit to children is immense. We just have to remember that diseases like measles can kill or allow a child to fall off a precipice leading to malnutrition, poor development or death. Polio can kill and cripple. I saw a child die of tetanus in Ethiopia, and that was enough to vastly increase my enthusiasm for immunizing children.

Promotion of breastfeeding:

In America some of the aisles of our supermarkets are filled with an array of options for bottled and powdered mixtures called "formula" that we can use to feed infants. It is a viable and sometimes a preferable option to bottle feed our babies. For the most part, there is a relatively low risk of bottle fed babies in an industrialized country being serious harmed by drinking from a bottle. It seems that breast feeding is an option for many mothers. In contrast to this, in an impoverished country like Ethiopia, breast feeding is a matter of life and death for young children. To state it another way, promoting breast feeding in the developing world is in fact, part and parcel of the "child revolution".

Think about the risk and the expense of trying to bottle feed a child in a poor country. There may be a lack of clean and safe water to begin with. There may be no means to sterilize and clean bottles adequately. The formula may not be mixed properly and may be diluted to an unacceptable degree.

The expense of bottles, and formula, along with a lack of clean water make the notion of bottle feeding in a poor country untenable. Such a method of feeding an infant was to a large degree unthinkable. Breast feeding was and is crucial to the survival and well-being of children in a country like Ethiopia.

Breast milk is associated with lower rates of illness, and malnutrition among vulnerable children. Breast milk gives complete balanced nutrition and can be used as the sole source of feeding for about the first six months of a child's life. After that, soft foods that an infant can consume should be used. Breast milk gives the child antibodies that help fight off infection. By contrast bottle feeding in a setting of a dearth of clean water, lack of refrigeration, and poverty creates a life-threatening milieu for a young child.

It must be kept in mind that the HIV/AIDS pandemic has currently made breast feeding more challenging. This is because a mother can transmit the HIV virus to her young child by breast feeding. In fact, if no anti-HIV drugs (which are used to treat/prevent HIV infection, are taken while breast feeding, the risk of a baby getting infected is high and as much as 45%). If medications are taken correctly during pregnancy and during breastfeeding, the HIV infection rate can be reduced to about 5%.

HIV infection was not an issue when I was living and working in Ethiopia as the pandemic levels had not been realized or discussed while I was in-country. It is a crisis now.

Medical supervision must be done to prevent mother to child transmission of HIV

Besides the information on specific information to benefit the health and welfare of mothers and children, I paid attention to the demographics and statistical information noted in the State of the World's Children reports. There was information available such as: infant mortality rate, total population, child population, GNP per capita, life expectancy, adult literacy, school enrollment, and income distribution. These were referred to as "basic indicators"

Other statistics included:

1) <u>Nutrition</u>: Low birth weight, breast feeding, malnutrition, food production and calorie intake.

2) Health: Access to clean water, immunization of children, immunization of mothers, life expectancy.

3) Education: Male and female literacy, primary school enrollment, secondary school enrollment.

4) <u>Demographic Indicators</u>: Infant deaths, child deaths, overall death rate, birth rate, fertility rate, population growth

5) Economic Indicators: GNP per capita, growth rate, inflation, poverty, urbanization.

There were some important definitions as follows:

> Infant mortality rate: annual number of deaths of infant under one year of age per 1,000 live births
>
> Child death rate: annual number of deaths of children aged 1-4 years per 1,000 population in same age group

Oddly enough, the statistical figure that caught my eye the most was the infant mortality rate. I came to believe that this figure alone was a snapshot of the well-being of a nation and its children. Ethiopia in the report ranked number 13 in the world in infant mortality and was in a group of nations considered to have a "very high" infant mortality rate, that is greater than 100 per 1,000 live births. This tells us that much work needed to be done to improve the health and welfare of mothers and children and indeed the general health status of the country. This was my feeling when I was an expatriate living in Ethiopia.

If I were to return to Ethiopia, I would focus my attention to helping those who were the focus of the report discussed, and I would also focus on helping out in regards to the HIV pandemic. Perhaps one day this sentiment might become reality. I am grateful to this day for the UNICEF report which turned out to be such a source of solace and information. I was not able to implement the strategies therein given the situation in Ethiopia when I was there, but it is awesome to know there is an efficacious approach available.

Mission to America

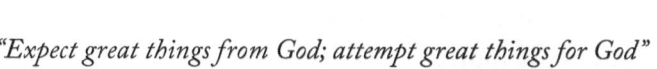

"Expect great things from God; attempt great things for God"
William Carey

Our stay in Ethiopia was not quite what we expected it to be. We had no idea that we would be separated for a total of 8-9 months, with the bulk of the time spent in Makale (6 months total). From the standpoint of my wife and me, we were disappointed that we could not do more to help those most in need-and that was those affected most by the famine, which were children. In addition, I wish we had received more food, blankets, medicine, and clothing for distribution. I wish we had more doctors and nurses to help. I wish we had received more of the proper and appropriate medical supplies, and medication. I wish I had had more training and guidance in how to run the medical facilities there, and how to get funding to help improve them. I was also compelled by the images in my mind of what I had seen in the media prior to coming to the country and what I had seen with my own eyes, and this made me do what I thought needed to be done despite the consequences. We had made a commitment originally to work in Ethiopia for my church for six years, but my wife and I decided that at mid-term which was the 3-year mark, it was time to leave and go back home.

In about a month after arriving back in Denver, Colorado a friend of mine; (who was a clinic administrator) arranged and in fact, called me to work at an Internal Medicine clinic to fill in for a physician who was on maternity leave. This lead to a nearly 22-year period of service with Kaiser (the Colorado Permanente Medical Group) until my retirement (which turned out to be temporary!) I worked as a full-time physician in the department of internal medicine, in the Denver Metro area, from 1987-2009.

I believe now that what I have as a result of my tour in Ethiopia is a form of PTSD (Post traumatic stress disorder). It did not make me dysfunctional, as it might with some people. I was left first of all with indelible memories of things that happened. I can still see in my mind the faces of those I treated in the clinics, and our hospital at Gimbie. I remember those who passed away despite my efforts. I remember the patients and family member who thanked me when a life was spared. They were the poorest of the poor, and there were few if any witnesses to their outpouring of thanks. I remember the joy and gratification of giving out food, blankets, and medicine to those in need. I remember the expatriate workers and Ethiopians I worked with. The treatment for my PTSD was not to take a medication but to do health ministry in my community separate from my work as an internist in a clinic. The satisfaction and gratification were as good as taking Prozac or some other drug. To this day I have flashbacks of the things that happened in Ethiopia, and I will be living with those memories for the rest of my life. My wife and I were never the same as a result of the things we experienced.

One of the most crucial concepts that developed in our minds is that our jobs in America were more than just a means to earn a livelihood, they were a mission. The way I saw things is that our task was to help people find physical, spiritual, and mental healing. My wife was trained as an LPN prior to our marriage and after our return to America, she completed her training as an RN in

1992. This enhanced our attempts to do the work we had to do. We together developed a two-fold approach to our work which included employment to earn a livelihood as well as work through our church, the Park Hill Seventh-day Adventist Church, in Denver. We also developed relationships with many people and agencies in our community to do community outreach.

It was to a large degree a letdown to come back and to live and work in America. Despite the challenges and frustration, it was immensely rewarding to be a missionary. We had to find a substitute for that. Our first task was to focus our attention on our jobs. My wife worked part time as a congregational nurse with a local organization: The Metro Denver Black Church Initiative, which later became the Center for African American Health in Denver. I was employed as a full-time physician with the Colorado Permanente Medical Group (Kaiser Permanente). I worked at a clinic in Denver. I was also on the staff at Exempla Saint Joseph Hospital. I was a full-time internist in the clinic and a part time hospital physician. This full time medical work took the bulk of my time and energies, but in addition on weekends, and evenings, there was work in the church and community to be done.

Not long after I began my work in Denver as an internal medicine physician, I encountered a daunting and life-transforming task- taking care of patients infected with the HIV virus.

We know today that the African subcontinent is the epicenter of the AIDS pandemic. Oddly enough, during my stay in Ethiopia 1984-1987, I did not see even one case of HIV infection or AIDS. (I discovered in retrospect that the first HIV infections were identified in Ethiopia in 1984, and first AIDS cases reported in 1986.) Because of my not dealing with HIV infection, I did not get any experience while laboring as a missionary in Africa in regards to treating HIV infection or AIDS. However, after starting my work in America as a physician, I learned quickly what I needed to know. Admittedly, in 1987, the state of the art was that there was far too little we could do, and few drugs to attack the HIV virus itself. Since the first description of "human immunodeficiency virus" infection in 1981, until I arrived on the scene in 1987, there had been too little progress in my view, to help people with HIV infection and AIDS.

I had to first go through a major paradigm shift and a change in my thinking about taking care of HIV infected patients in general, and gay men in particular. Sad to say, my initial reaction to these patients was a significant reticence to treat them. I realized that I was inappropriately prejudiced against them. It is tragic to note that I was prejudiced because of my religious beliefs. I had heard from the pulpit in church, and from Christian literature I had read that people who were HIV infected were essentially getting what they deserved. However, I was obligated to treat these patients as they were coming to my clinic in droves to see me and my fellow internists. Unless I wanted to quit my job, I had to treat them. I then felt ashamed and dismayed at my judgment as it was not consistent with how Jesus would treat people, and it was unacceptable thinking for a Christian in my view. I rapidly decided that the appropriate thing for me to do was to show all the compassion and wisdom I could to help these people, with God's help. I threw myself without reservation into the task at hand.

There is no question that today AIDS is a dreadful affliction. It seemed more dreadful in terms of my personal experience and involvement with patient care beginning in 1987. The treatment options were far more limited in scope at that time, and treatment then did not prevent an enormous burden of suffering and death. It seemed that from the time of diagnosis until death of patients with HIV infection there was an inexorable downhill course which was painful for patients, their families, and medical care providers.

We medical providers had a carefully crafted body of information about what the HIV virus did to the body, criteria for diagnosis, the imposing list of "opportunistic" infections and cancers, and available drug therapies. We had quick access to medical information on the internet, and in print. We had infectious disease consultants to help guide us and I spoke to them frequently. We had a team of people to help including nurses, and social workers. We unfortunately became all too familiar with taking care of people who were terminally ill.

Giving good care to HIV infected patients required meticulous care with careful attention to detail. Medical providers also had to be concerned about the social and economic situation our patients were in: where they lived, who lived with them, financial resources, and insurance coverage.

I saw a repeated scenario played out again and again with HIV infection. First of all, many of those infected presented to us already acutely ill. They came to us with fever, enlarged lymph glands (mostly in the neck), sore mouths and throats with night sweats, diarrhea, weight loss, rashes, cough, shortness of breath, among other symptoms. We did the obligatory lab tests, but the results were a foregone conclusion. Those with obvious symptoms already had advanced disease. They were at risk due to unprotected heterosexual or homosexual sex. Some had been intravenous drug users and had shared needles with someone. Many, if not all had some ominous findings on physical examination. One of the most striking findings was "oral thrush" which was a fungal infection of the mouth and throat, which sometimes involved the esophagus. The patient would have a thick white coating of the oral cavity along with painful swallowing. They might have reddish purple spots on the face and body which was actually a type of skin cancer designated Kaposi's sarcoma. This skin cancer was uncontrollable by treatment methods we had and in some produced large disfiguring skin lesions and death. Some presented with a parasite infecting the lungs with the name pneumocystis carinii and would present very short of breath, with low blood oxygen levels, and very abnormal chest x-rays. Those with this lung infection required hospital admission for treatment with intravenous medication and oxygen.

There were those who presented with intractable diarrhea, and horrific weight loss. All told it seemed as if there was just a legion of potential infections and cancer due to an immune system that was just not functioning. It was possible for one individual to have more than one contagion in addition to the malignancy Kaposi's sarcoma. We had to do a complete catalog as it were of a patient's ailments and we might come up with a dreadful and distressing list. These afflictions were referred to as "opportunistic infections" related to the fact that the HIV virus caused an immune surveillance system that did not protect one against infections and cancers that would not ordinarily occur. We tried to treat these disorders but all too frequently we found that at times it was a toss-up as to which was worse: the treatment or the disease. The side effects of the powerful intravenous and oral drugs were at times intolerable and dangerous.

We had regimens of what we called prophylactic treatments intended to prevent certain opportunistic infections although at times some of these medications were also not tolerated well. We had no choice but to make the efforts to prevent these infections. These preventive medications were given to most people if possible, and this might include those who were found to be HIV positive, but not yet acutely ill.

When I began my work with those infected with HIV in 1987, there was a drug found to help to a degree: zidovudine or AZT. It was a drug called an antiretroviral drug that inhibited to a degree the HIV virus rather than the infections it caused. It had previously been used to treat cancer patients. It was the only drug we had to directly attack the virus. The truth of the matter was that AZT in my view was a huge disappointment. It did not stop the inexorable downhill course of our HIV infected patients. It had at times intolerable side effects and many just could not tolerate even a reduced dose of AZT. We had criteria for its use, we knew all of the potential issues in terms of side effects and interaction with other drugs, but still, I was dismayed that AZT seemed to help far too little.

HIV infection was in my view like a perfect storm to produce an immense amount of suffering for those infected. It was painful to take care of those infected. Health care providers knew that the diagnosis of HIV infection in 1987 and for some years afterward was essentially a death sentence, and this was true worldwide. There were a few fortunate long-term survivors who still live today, but this was the exception. That was the state of affairs until a breakthrough occurred.

At this point in time we do not have a cure or a vaccine for HIV infection. However, we do have treatment that can change a disease with a rapid death sentence into a manageable condition with a longer-term survival and a better quality of life. The more effective treatment regimen was developed and started in the mid-1990's. The regimen is called: "highly active anti-retroviral therapy" or HAART. Medications were found that more effectively combat the HIV virus directly. I suspect that many in our nation and elsewhere are not aware of how efficacious these medications are now. The medication groups have imposing names: nucleoside reverse transcriptase inhibitors, integrase inhibitors, protease inhibitors and others. The medications are given now as combination therapy with two to three drugs given together. Pills have been developed that contain as many as three different medications, and also pills that can be given just once daily. HIV infected patients now have a much smaller pill burden to consume. In addition, medications can be taken prior to exposure to prevent infection if one is exposed. There are drugs that can prevent pregnant and breast-feeding mothers from passing the infection to their babies. Those at risk are strongly advised to seek screening and treatment and discussion of all options.

The considerations in choices of anti-HIV medications is complex now. A medical provider gives one group of medications to those never treated and other groups to those who have been treated before, but perhaps not responding as they should due to growing resistance of the virus. Providers have to be wary of drug interactions, and side effects which are many. There are more than 20 drugs to use, in 6 different classes. The regimens take some skill and experience to administer. This explains why the people who give these medications now are often infectious disease specialists or very experienced primary care doctors.

In addition to the anti-retroviral medications, patients also may receive medications to prevent the dreaded infections that can occur due to a malfunctioning immune system. Certain immunizations need to be given to prevent infections. Patients need to be screened for sexually transmitted diseases if needed. Lab surveillance needs to be done to gauge the effectiveness of treatment and to allow for early detection of unwanted harmful drug side effects. There are also concerns about any co-existing or pre-existing conditions such as high blood pressure, heart disease, diabetes, kidney disease and liver disease.

There are concerns now that those who live a lot longer with HIV infection may succumb to the usual diseases of middle and older age such as heart disease, and strokes. Indeed, some of the medications used to treat HIV infections may in fact cause elevation in cholesterol levels. Habits such as smoking, illicit drug use and alcohol abuse are even more harmful in the face of the medications that have to be given, with the attendant risks involved.

All things considered, HIV infected patients can now live much longer and better than when I returned to America in 1987. The disease is not curable but thank God there is more we can do and much suffering can and has been averted. However, think for a moment about those in our country and across the planet who do not have access to the care described. In addition, there are millions who are infected, but do not know it worldwide, and serve as a reservoir of spreading the disease. The suffering due to HIV infection has not gone away, just like famine, and malnutrition in an impoverished third world country. One tragedy we see is the lack of information, misinformation, and complacency about the pandemic. Make no mistake about it, HIV infection is not a warm and fuzzy topic. We do not want to talk about it or hear about it. The stigma is still huge for those infected and for those at high risk for getting infected. There is therefore much preventable death and suffering today. I see a parallel in my mind: treating a severely malnourished child in Africa and a thin wasted individual with advanced AIDS (fortunately I have not seen the latter for years.) I have the same emotional reaction in both scenarios. The problem is not going away and there is much we can do to help if we have the will and courage to do so.

I came to highly value the great diversity of patients I encountered while in full time medical practice. I saw people from every corner of the globe, and countless walks of life. Being an internal medicine physician, I had to help patients and their families cope with a gamut of illnesses from the trivial to the life-threatening. However, one underlying incessant reality I observed is how much of the illness and concomitant suffering I saw was preventable. Of course, there were those who lived a healthy lifestyle and still had devastating illnesses. There were also those who just had an unfortunate genetic profile and this was part and parcel of a catastrophic illness. Nevertheless, for the most part, cause and effect was a reality I saw. Unhealthy lifestyles, addictions, and poor choices produced a predictable harvest of suffering and pain that did not have to happen. Even with good insurance and good access to health care, toxic lifestyles could trump the efforts of the best medical practioners.

At times when trying to give counsel to patients about changing habits, I have had people say to me: "Well doc, you know we all have to die of something!" My response to this is two observations.

First of all, it is possible to die decades before one's time, and this happens all too frequently. Secondly, a person may live to old age in the 70's, 80's or older, but spend the last years of life in misery, and pain with a multitude of medications, multiple chronic illnesses, and frequent hospital admissions. These are tragedies that may not have to happen. We are in fact going to die from something, but we should have a keen interest in avoiding unnecessary grief and agony!

There are those in our country who are uninsured and underinsured. Many people have access to care but do not even go to be seen for medical care when needed. Some due to lack of motivation or even denial make it difficult to manage conditions such as diabetes, high blood pressure, and heart disease. Individuals in our society think that if they feel well there is no need to live a healthier lifestyle. There is a lack of understanding or assenting to the fact that there is lurking about undetected conditions that can bear an immense burden of preventable affliction. One can have cancer, diabetes, heart disease, HIV infection, sexually transmitted disease, hypertension, liver disease, and kidney disease to name a few and still feel perfectly well, for a time that is. Despite all of the information available in print and on the internet, there is a pressing need to do education of the public to inform and to motivate. All of these observations compelled me to act. However, there was another compelling impetus to act. I was and to this day still haunted by the memories of caring for famine victims in Ethiopia. Those were people in need who I could help, and I did all in my power to help. However, there are people right here in America, and in my own community who need help as well to live longer and better. Because of this my wife and I came to still view ourselves as missionaries, but to our own country. This lead to a lot of work outside of the confines of our "regular" jobs.

One of our early outreach projects was what we called an "HIV/AIDS support group". We attempted this in the early 1990s. Our aim was to hold a weekly meeting with those infected by HIV, their family members/significant others and people who just wanted to learn about HIV/AIDS. This was attempted about 2-3 years prior to the breakthrough in more efficacious treatment for HIV infection. We tried diligently to send out flyers and make phone calls to potentially interested individuals. We did meet with about 2-4 people, but eventually it was just me and my wife sitting in the basement of our church waiting for someone else to show up. Finally, after one month or so, we abandoned further efforts for the support group. It did not however end our efforts to help people with HIV infection. I did do an Email campaign and spoke at various public venues when possible giving PowerPoint presentations on the topic. We decided to do whatever we could to help people with this affliction.

One encouraging and rewarding event that did happen is that a door opened for me to do health education through a local newspaper published in the Denver Metro area, and later in Aurora, Boulder, Colorado Springs and Pueblo, Colorado. This newspaper is called *The Body of Christ News*. It is sent free of charge to many churches, and businesses in the cities noted, with a special focus on the African American community. I started writing a health column for this publication monthly in 1995 and this continues to the present. I have tried to address the major health issues of our times such as AIDS, diabetes, hypertension, obesity, cancer, stroke, hypertension, depression, stress and others. The publisher Randy McCowan has been supportive and awesome to work with. I trust that the readers have benefitted.

My wife and I got involved in health screening in our community. We participated in health fairs at our church, other churches in the community as well as various community centers. We also went to other venues such as libraries, shopping centers, and salons, and barber shops. For more than 20 years we have participated in the Denver (now Colorado) Black Arts Festival, doing blood pressure screening and health education for about 500 or many more people during the three days of the festival. We also have participated in the annual Juneteenth celebration doing a similar outreach. For a period of 10 years, we conducted the "Nine Health Fair" at our church which was an event conducted by a local television station. We found health screening and just talking with and meeting people immensely rewarding.

We developed a fond regard for collaborating and working with multiple agencies such as the following: The American Diabetes Association, the Alzheimer's Association, the Center for African American Health, the Colorado Black Health Collaborative, the Inner-City Health Center, and the Greater Denver Interfaith Alliance. From these organizations we received many thousands of dollars' worth of teaching material we could distribute to the public. We were thus empowered to go to multiple venues in the Denver metro area to do outreach and health ministry actually outside and in addition to my work as a clinic internist. We have also been able to visit multiple churches, and other venues, to do health education.

We have also worked outside of the Denver area with a national part of our church hierarchy-the North American Division of our church, and the Central States Conference-a Midwest church region.

One of our most gratifying projects is the Barbershop/Salon Health Outreach Project. We have 14 shops now we go to in the Denver Metro area and do 4-hour sessions of free blood pressure and diabetes screening to 1 to 2 of the shops, in turn almost weekly. My wife and I started thus outreach in 2008 and at first, we did it infrequently and it was just about every 2-3 months at the barbershop I have visited since being a junior at my local high school. In 2012 we formed a coalition with a group of other local Denver Metro area residents. We are now collaborating with a large group of volunteers with the Colorado Black Health Collaborative.

We have worked together up to the present in 2019. Together we have screened over 8,500 for high blood pressure, over 1600 for diabetes, and have amassed over 5,000 volunteer hours. We have referred the uninsured and those on Medicaid to the Inner City Health Center (a local safety net clinic) for needed medical care.

We are grateful beyond words to all of the many volunteers we have worked with and the churches and agencies we have collaborated with. We plan to continue our efforts as long as possible.

Working for the medical group I joined, and Exempla Saint Joseph Hospital as an internist was arduous and stressful. It was however, immensely rewarding. In fact, retiring (for a while) in 2009 was a very painful experience and to this day I miss my patients and my coworkers. (I did return to work part-time in geriatrics in 2012!) Getting involved in work in the church and community helped to fill the gap left in my time and focus after retirement.

I have tried to describe now what I am calling our "Mission to America". We feel compelled to do what we do because of our experiences in Ethiopia. We believe that what we are doing, we will continue to do as long as it is humanly possible.

Donor Fatigue

———— ❖ ————

"And let us not be weary in well-doing: for in due season we shall reap if we faint not"

Galatians 6:9

DURING THE SUMMER OF 2011, news outlets were focused on a famine in a region of Africa referred to as the Horn of Africa. This famine involved the countries of Somalia, Ethiopia, Kenya, Eritrea, and Djibouti. Graphic pictures of emaciated children and their thin parents were shown on the screen and in print. This famine was frequently the lead stories on news broadcasts. Appeals for funds were made to help those in need. What happened next was predictable. After about 1 month or so, the story largely faded from view and from the prominence it once had. In fact, there was no more mention of the crisis at all. Despite this the crisis was far from over. Granted there was political turmoil particularly in Somalia which is plagued by anarchy, and incomprehensible political violence. There exists in the Horn of Africa, and indeed other places on the continent enduring poverty, and hunger. Truth be told, there is always a famine somewhere on this planet, but we may be quite unaware of this.

In some corners of the globe, people live lives in the midst of squalor, misery, and poverty that are inconceivable to those of us who live in industrialized countries. There is always a crisis somewhere involving famine. Then there is talk of the millions of people impacted by mass starvation and a poignant appeal for food, money, and medical supplies. We see in print, on the internet and on television, pictures of those in need and those people on the scene trying to help to help and report the problem. At first there is a large outpouring of aid that may be worth millions of dollars. However, gradually the flow of money and goods declines noticeably. To be fair there may be some political concerns such as corrupt and repressive regime that may even divert aid to purchasing weapons or divert money to foreign bank accounts for misuse by those in power, and this is of course a legitimate concern. There may be huge logistical problems such as transportation glitches, and problems with distribution. There may be a sense of futility that despite heroic efforts to provide aid, the efforts are an act of futility as the crisis and the suffering continue unabated. What happens next is a diminution in the amount of aid sent and it may almost stop altogether.

However, just talk to those on the scene giving aid. They will tell you the needs are still enormous. This diminution in assistance and goods we can call "donor fatigue". It was a term I heard discussed in meetings for expatriates while in Ethiopia. There may be logical reasons for the fatigue but it is real. The ruling military junta, the despot and those in power may suffer not at all. Those who really suffer are those least able to defend themselves and that may be children and poor peasants. Our compassion and our willingness to help have their limits.

When you are an aid worker in a foreign land, and you are taking care of a desperately ill child in the throes of marasmus and suffering from pneumonia, and diarrhea, you have little thought for politics. What you want are the tools to help you give the care needed. You want to be able to provide food and shelter to those in need. As an aid worker, you are unable to change the political climate, although you may wish you could. Expatriates there to help may not even be direct witnesses to diversion and misuse of aid, and that was true for me. I simply tried to take care of all who came to me for help. It is in the purview of governments and perhaps large NGOs to push for political change, I could not push for such change, and continue to be allowed to work in a foreign country.

One thing we need to accept is that for the foreseeable future, there will always be a famine with all of the associated consequences somewhere on this planet. The question is, what do we do about it?

I wish we could make it our aim to do a better job of helping those in need despite the political and logistical challenges. I know there are dangers at times to life and limb if we chose to make such a commitment. Just think for a moment however, what would happen if a significant portion of the enormous sum of money worldwide spent for weapons and armies was devoted to feeding the hungry and helping those in need no matter where they may be. Worldwide military spending is in the trillion-dollar range and will likely only increase. Imagine that we never develop fatigue when it comes to spending the money needed to give aid and are relentless in our assistance. I think the world would be a better place and much preventable death and suffering would be extinguished. It is just a thought, and a subject of a prayer of mine.

BIBLIOGRAPHY

"East African Famine, Somalia, 2011" *The New York Times* http://topics.nytimes.com/topics/reference/timestopics/subjects/f/famine/index.html

"USAID on Culture Shock" http://www.ccfrussia.ru/?mod=s_page&sp_id=106

Ofcansky, Thomas P and Laverle Bercy, *Ethiopia a Country Study*. Washington: GPO for the Library of Congress. 1991.

Garbus, Lisa. *HIV/AIDS in Ethiopia*. San Francisco, California: AIDS Policy Research Center University of California, 2003.

Global Humanitarian Assistance Report 2018

Office on Women's Health Women's Health. Gov Pregnancy and HIV

Grant, James P. "The State of the World's Children 1984." 1984

"Morbidity and Mortality Weekly Report First Report of AIDS." June 1, 2001, Volume 50, No. 21:430.

Hodes, Richard MD, and Helmut Kloos, Phd. "Health and Medical Care in Ethiopia." *New England Journal of Medicine* (Oct. 6, 1988 Vol. 319, No. 14): 918-924.

Selik, Richard M, Susan Y. Chu, and John W. Ward MD. "Trends in Infectious Disease and Cancer among persons dying of HIV in the United States from 1987-1992," *Annals of Internal Medicine* (15 Dec 1995 Vol. 123 No. 12): 933-936

Milner, Kate. "Flashback 1984: Portrait of a Famine." *BBC News* April 6, 2000, http://news.bbc.co.uk/2/hi/africa/703958.stm.

"Immigrants and Expatriates by Caroline Penn." http://www.the-travel-doctor.com/expatriates.htm

www.ingramcontent.com/pod-product-compliance
Lightning Source LLC
LaVergne TN
LVHW040153080526
838202LV00042B/3141